GLOBAL VIEWS

A MULTICULTURAL READER
WITH
LANGUAGE EXERCISES

Jeanne Becijos

Dominie Press, Inc.

Publisher: Raymond Yuen

Copy Editor: Becky Colgan

Illustrator: Tony Greven

Graphic Design: Sci-Tech Communication Services

Cover Designer: Steven Morris

Dominie Press, Inc.
5945 Pacific Center Boulevard, Suite 505
San Diego, California 92121 USA

ISBN 1-56270-438-9
Printed in Singapore by PH Productions
1 2 3 4 5 6 7 C 99 98 97 96 95

Table of Contents

Photo Acknowledgments

Unit 1, page 1, Embassy of France

Unit 2, page 4, Japan National Tourist Organization

Unit 12, page 34, Owen Franken/German Information Center

Unit 16, page 46, Embassy of Israel

Unit 17, page 49, Embassy of Russia

Unit 19, page 45, Hawaii Visitors Bureau

Unit 22, page 65, Embassy of the Czech Republic

The World

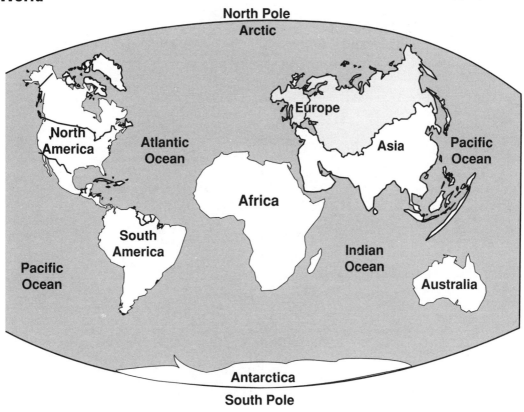

Africa

North America

United States
(Alaska)

Greenland

Canada

United States

Mexico

South America

Venezuela

Guyana

Suriname

Colombia

French Guyana

Ecuador

Brazil

Peru

Bolivia

Paraguay

Chile

Argentina

Uruguay

Europe

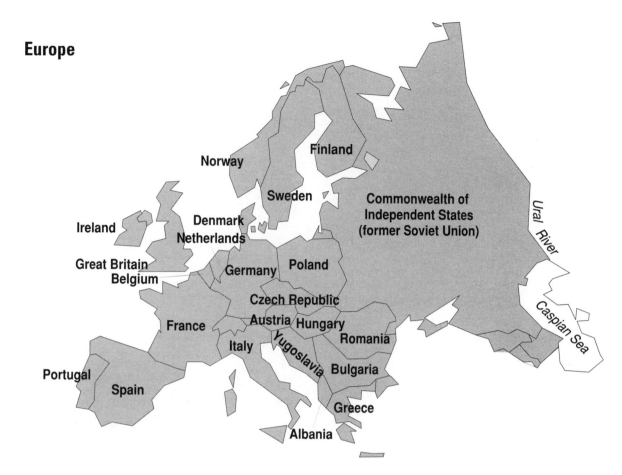

Norway

Finland

Sweden

Ireland

Denmark
Netherlands

Commonwealth of
Independent States
(former Soviet Union)

Ural River

Great Britain
Belgium

Germany

Poland

Caspian Sea

Czech Republic

France

Austria Hungary

Romania

Italy

Yugoslavia

Bulgaria

Portugal

Spain

Greece

Albania

Asia

Commonwealth of
Independent States
(former Soviet Union

Japan

Syria
Lebanon

Turkey

Caspian Sea

China

Israel
Jordan

Iraq

Saudi
Arabia

Iran

Afghanistan

Philippines

Pakistan

Nepal

Southern Yemen

Oman

India

Myanmar

Vietnam

New Guinea

Thailand

Cambodia

Malaysia

Indonesia

Sri Lanka

Australia

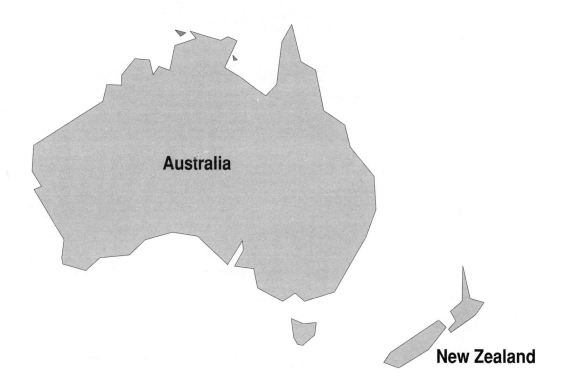

Australia

New Zealand

Antarctica

Antarctica

Introduction to the Teacher

Global Views is a multicultural reader with language exercises. The reading material contains biographies, holidays, folktales, and descriptions of people and places from representative areas around the world. The readings and exercises are appropriate for ESL and bilingual students in elementary grades, junior high, high school, and adult basic education. The text provides interesting and motivating reading for beginning ESL students.

Each reading selection is introduced with geographic questions followed by grammar and language information that relates to the reading topic. The reading level and grammar exercises are sequenced in order of difficulty, with basic reading and grammar in the beginning of the book. The units may be completed in class or used as homework assignments. If the units are given as homework assignments, you may wish to practice the grammar and language information in class before students complete the work at home.

The value of learning grammar and language is primarily to provide the students with rules to correct their writing and to better understand their reading. This knowledge is valuable in preparing students for advanced academic courses. As the grammar and language are presented in context, the students see language as it occurs naturally. While the students are improving their language skills, they are also learning valuable information about people and countries from across the globe.

To facilitate instruction of the material, use the following information and teaching suggestions to correlate with each section of the unit.

Introduction

Each reading selection is introduced with questions regarding the geographic location of the country involved, including the name of the continent and bordering countries. Students may look up the answers on maps provided in the front of the book, or you can point out each country on a globe or large map with the whole class. You may wish to review the continents and major countries with the class before you start the book. Following the geographic questions is a question that relates to a vocabulary term or a concept in the reading. This prereading question will help the students to better understand the reading selection.

Reading Selection and Questions

The reading selections include biographies, holidays, folktales, and descriptions of people and places from representative areas all around the world. Each reading selection is followed by comprehension questions to check for understanding. You or a student may read the selection aloud, or students can read the selection silently and answer the questions alone, with a partner, or in a small group.

Grammar Exercise

The grammar exercises explain various points of grammar that are utilized in the reading selections. The exercises that follow practice the grammar point and review the information learned in the reading selection at the same time. You may introduce the grammar on the board, along with additional exercises, to further clarify the lesson. Students may answer the questions alone, with a partner, or in a small group.

Language Exercise

Following the grammar exercise is a language exercise, again relating to the reading topic. Included are exercises on capitalization, punctuation, spelling rules, vocabulary, and other information related to learning a language. You may want to give additional examples on the board. Students may answer the questions alone, with a partner, or in a small group.

Extra Practice

Each unit ends with extra practice that gives students an additional chance to practice language. The questions relate to the students' own personal lives. Students again may answer the questions alone, with a partner, or in a small group.

Unit 1

Introduction

1. The seven continents are North America, South America, Africa, Europe, Asia, Australia, and Antarctica. On which continent is France?

2. Name two countries that border on France.

3. The Eiffel Tower is a famous place. What is a famous place in your country?

Story

"The Eiffel Tower" tells of a famous place in France.

The Eiffel Tower

My family and I are from Spain. We visit France in the summer. We always see Paris. Alicia likes the museums in Paris. Juan likes the girls. I like the Eiffel Tower. My parents like everything.

The Eiffel Tower

Questions

1. Where is Paris?
2. Where is the Eiffel Tower?
3. What does Alicia like?

Grammar Exercise

Study the grammar explanation below. Then follow the directions.

Verbs: Simple Present		
I We You/They	visit see like	France.
He She It	visits sees likes	France.

Directions: Copy each sentence. Choose the correct verb. Mark the sentence as true or false according to the story.

Example: We (visit) (visits) France in the summer.   **True   False**
              We _visit_ France in the summer.   True

1. We always (see) (sees) Paris.   **True   False**
2. My sister's name is Alicia. She (visit) (visits) France.   **True   False**
3. She (like) (likes) the Eiffel Tower the best.   **True   False**
4. My brother's name is Juan. He (see) (sees) Paris.   **True   False**
5. He (like) (likes) girls the best.   **True   False**
6. I always (see) (sees) Paris.   **True   False**
7. I (like) (likes) museums the best.   **True   False**
8. My father and mother are my parents. They (like) (likes) everything. **True   False**

2

Language Exercise

Read the information about capitalization. Then follow the directions.

Capitalization: First Word in a Sentence
Capital Letters: A B C D E F G H I J K L M N O P Q R S T U V W X Y Z
Small Letters: a b c d e f g h i j k l m n o p q r s t u v w x y z
Each new sentence starts with a capital letter. For example:
My family and I are from Spain. We visit France in the summer.

Directions: Copy the sentences. Start each sentence with a capital letter.

Example: my sister likes museums. my bother likes girls.
             My sister likes museums. My brother likes girls.

the Eiffel Tower is in Paris, France. it was built in 1889. the tower was designed by Alexander Eiffel, a French engineer. the metal tower is 984 feet high. it was the highest building in the world until 1930. at first people didn't like the tower. now it is a famous place in Paris.

Extra Practice

Write the names of places you visit. Ask other people the names of places they visit.

Example: I visit Texas. Julia visits Los Angeles.

Unit 2

Introduction

1. The seven continents are North America, South America, Africa, Europe, Asia, Australia, and Antarctica. What continent is Japan near?
2. Name two countries that are near Japan.
3. Christmas is a holiday. Write the names of two other holidays.

Story

"Favorite Holidays in Japan" tells of three holidays in Japan.

Favorite Holidays in Japan

The teacher is talking to two children. Akane is a girl, and Takeo is a boy.

Teacher: What holiday do you like?

Akane: I like *Hina Matsuri*. This is the girls' Doll Festival. It is on March 3.

Teacher: What holiday do you like, Takeo?

Takeo: I like *Kodomo-no-Hi*. It is Children's Day. It is on May 5.

Akane: I like *Kodomo-no-Hi,* too. We fly kites.

Teacher: What holiday do your parents like?

Takeo: They like *Taiiku-no-Hi* on October 10. It is a day for sports.

Hina Matsuri,
the Doll Festival

Questions

1. What holiday is for girls?
2. What holiday do Takeo and Akane like?
3. Which Japanese holiday do you like?

Grammar Exercise

Study the grammar explanation. Then follow the directions.

Personal Pronouns	
I	
you	
he	= one male (for example, brother, boy, man, father)
she	= one female (for example, sister, girl, woman, mother)
it	= one
we	= I + one or more
they	= two or more

Directions: Copy each sentence. Replace the underlined words with the personal pronouns **I**, **you**, **he**, **she**, **it**, **we**, or **they**. Mark the sentences true or false, according to the story.

Example: Takeo is a boy.   **True**   **False**
             He is a boy.   True

1. Akane is a girl.   **True**   **False**

2. Takeo and Akane like the Doll Festival.   **True**   **False**

3. Girls like the Doll Festival.   **True**   **False**

4. Akane likes no holiday.   **True**   **False**

5. Takeo likes Children's Day.   **True**   **False**

6. Children's Day is on March 3.   **True**   **False**

7. The parents like *Taiiku-no-Hi*.   **True**   **False**

8. *Taiiku-no-Hi* is on October 10.   **True**   **False**

Language Exercise

Read the information about indentation. Then follow the directions.

Indentation
Indent at the beginning of a new paragraph.
(Indent = go in 5 spaces).
Example:
Akane and Takeo are Japanese. They like holidays. Akane's favorite holiday is the Doll Festival.

Directions: Copy the paragraphs below. Indent for a new paragraph when you see an asterisk (*).

Example: *Takeo's favorite holiday is Children's Day. He likes to fly kites.
     Takeo's favorite holiday is Children's Day. He likes to fly kites.

*All Japanese children like Children's Day. This holiday is on May 5. On this day, families fly a fish kite in the garden. *Hina Matsuri* is a special day for girls in Japan. This day is on March 3. On Doll Festival day, most girls put out 15 dolls. Girls visit their friends on this day.

Extra Practice

Write about things your family likes. Use the personal pronouns **I**, **you**, **he**, **she**, **it**, **we**, **they**.

Example: I like chocolate. He likes pizza.

Unit 3

Introduction

1. The seven continents are North America, South America, Africa, Europe, Asia, Australia, and Antarctica. What continent is the Philippines near?
2. Name two countries that are near the Philippines.
3. Do you celebrate Christmas? Explain.

Story

"Christmas in the Philippines" is a story about a special holiday.

Christmas in the Philippines

In many parts of the world, Christians celebrate Christmas. It is for the birth of Jesus Christ. Christmas is on December 25.

Christmas lasts many days in the Philippines. It begins nine days before Christmas on December 16. It ends January 6. Christmas Eve is the night of December 24. On Christmas Eve, singers sing Christmas songs in the streets. Boys and girls are at home on Christmas Eve. They put their shoes in the windows. In the morning, sweets and presents are inside their shoes.

Questions

1. When is Christmas?
2. What do singers do on the streets in the Philippines?
3. In the morning, what is inside the shoes?

Grammar Exercise

Study the grammar explanation. Then follow the directions.

Singular and Plural Nouns
Singular noun: one person, place, or thing
Examples: girl, shoe, street, home
Plural noun: two or more persons, places, or things
Examples: girls, shoes, streets, homes

Directions: Make the following nouns plural by adding s.

Example: part
parts

1. day
2. singer
3. song
4. boy

5. shoe
6. window
7. home
8. present

Directions: Copy the sentences. Choose the plural noun that makes the sentence correct.

Example: Christmas is celebrated in many (parts) (boys) of the world.
Christmas is celebrated in many _parts_ of the world.

1. (Christians) (Worlds) celebrate Christmas.
2. In the Philippines, Christmas lasts ten (weeks) (days).
3. On Christmas Eve, singers sing (girls) (songs).
4. The singers sing in the (streets) (shoes).
5. The boys and (girls) (days) are at home.

6. The boys and girls put their shoes in the (doors) (windows).

7. In the morning, the shoes have (songs) (presents) inside.

8. Also, the shoes have (windows) (sweets) inside.

Language Exercise

Read the information about alphabetical order. Then follow the directions.

Alphabetical Order
Words in alphabetical order are in order by their letters.

- Here is the alphabet:

  a b c d e f g h i j k l m n o p q r s t u v w x y z

- These words are in alphabetical order:

  boys   days   girls   nights   windows

- The following words start with the same letter. They are in order by the next letters in the words.

  shoes   songs   stops   streets   sweets

Directions: Write these words in alphabetical order:

| parts | world | days | ends | night |
| sing | boys | girls | windows | morning |

Now write these words in alphabetical order:

| boys | birth | begins | before | Christians |
| Christmas | singers | songs | shoes | streets |

Extra Practice

Write the names of ten foods that you like. Then write them in alphabetical order.

Unit 4

Introduction

1. The seven continents are North America, South America, Africa, Europe, Asia, Australia, and Antarctica. What continent is New Zealand near?
2. Name two countries that are near New Zealand.
3. What is a biography?

Story

"Edmund Hillary" is a biography of a famous explorer from New Zealand.

Edmund Hillary

Edmund Hillary is a famous explorer. He and Tensing Norkay, from Nepal, were the first to climb to the top of Mount Everest. Asia's Mount Everest is the highest mountain in the world.

Hillary was born in New Zealand on July 20, 1919. He first climbed mountains as a teenager. He and Norkay reached the top of Mount Everest on May 29, 1953. Norkay got an award from Great Britain for his work.

Hillary also went on an Antarctic expedition. He reached the South Pole on January 4, 1958. In 1975, Hillary wrote a book about his life.

Questions

1. What did Edmund Hillary and Tensing Norkay do?
2. Where is Mount Everest?
3. Do you like to climb mountains?

Grammar Exercise

Study the grammar explanation. Then follow the directions.

Indefinite Articles: a / an
a / an = one
• Use **a** or **an** with a singular noun.   • Use **a** before a word beginning with a consonant.   • Use **an** before a word beginning with a vowel (a, e, i, o, u) or vowel sound.   Examples: a mountain, an award, an hour

Directions: Copy each sentence. Complete the sentences with **a** or **an**. Mark the sentence as true or false, according to the story.

Example:	Hillary is (a / an) explorer.	**True**	**False**
	Hillary is _an_ explorer.	True	

1. Hillary and Norkay climbed (a / an) mountain.   **True**   **False**
2. They climbed Mount Everest in (a / an) hour.   **True**   **False**
3. Hillary is (a / an) man from Nepal.   **True**   **False**
4. Norkay is (a / an) Englishman.   **True**   **False**
5. Hillary first climbed mountains as (a / an) teenager.   **True**   **False**
6. Norkay got (a / an) award.   **True**   **False**
7. During (a / an) Antarctic expedition, Hillary reached the South Pole. **True**   **False**
8. In 1975, Norkay wrote (a / an) book about his life.   **True**   **False**

Writing the Date

Read this information about writing the date. Then follow the directions.

Writing the Date
Here are two common ways to write the date:
Month Day Year
May 29, 1953
5/29/53
These are the months of the year:

1 = January	5 = May	9 = September
2 = February	6 = June	10 = October
3 = March	7 = July	11 = November
4 = April	8 = August	12 = December

Directions: Write these dates in number form.

Example: July 20, 1919
              7/20/19

1. May 29, 1953   5. December 12, 1989
2. January 4, 1958   6. April 1, 1990
3. September 25, 1975   7. June 14, 1992
4. February 7, 1982   8. November 24, 1993

Directions: Write these dates in word form.

1. 3/29/21   5. 2/13/72
2. 11/15/38   6. 1/3/81
3. 4/22/46   7. 9/5/89
4. 5/9/56   8. 6/28/93

Extra Practice

Ask five people their birth dates. Write these dates in word form and number form.

Unit 5

Introduction

1. The seven continents are North America, South America, Africa, Europe, Asia, Australia, and Antarctica. On which continent is Vietnam?
2. Name two countries that border on Vietnam.
3. What is a festival?

Story

"The Mid-Autumn Festival" tells about a holiday in Vietnam.

Mid-Autumn Festival

"I am My Hoa. I am from Vietnam," said the young woman. "You are interested in a Vietnamese holiday. My favorite holiday is the Mid-Autumn Festival. The moon is full on this day. We are happy at this time. The children are given toys. The toys are paper fish, boats, or dragons. We are busy making the house beautiful. All the children are in a parade. The parade leader is dressed as a lion."

Questions

1. What is My Hoa's favorite holiday?
2. Describe the toys.
3. Do you like parades?

Grammar Exercise

Study the grammar explanation. Then follow the directions.

Verb: to be
This is the form of the **present tense** of the verb *to be*:

I	am	
he she it	is	happy
we you they	are	

Directions: Copy each sentence. Replace the missing word with the correct form of the verb *to be*. Mark the sentence as true or false, according to the story.

Example: "I _____ My Hoa," said the young woman.   **True   False**
            "I _am_ My Hoa," said the young woman.   True

1. "I _____ from Cambodia," said My Hoa.   **True   False**

2. You _____ from England.   **True   False**

3. My Hoa's favorite holiday _____ Christmas.   **True   False**

4. The moon _____ new during Mid-Autumn Festival.   **True   False**

5. "We _____ sad on this day," said My Hoa.   **True   False**

6. The children _____ given toys.   **True   False**

7. The toys _____ cars, airplanes, or cats.   **True   False**

8. The children _____ in a parade.   **True   False**

9. The parade leader _____ dressed as a lion.   **True   False**

Language Exercise

Read the information about contractions. Then follow the directions.

Contractions: with *to be*

• **Contractions** are two words joined together.
 	
• An **apostrophe** (') is put in place of the missing letter.
 	
    I am   = I'm   we are = we're
    she is = she's   you are = you're
    he is   = he's   they are = they're
    it is   = it's
 	
Example: **We're** happy during the Mid-Autumn Festival.

Directions: Replace the words in italics with the correct contractions. Then draw a picture of the feeling.

Example: *I am* scared.
              <u>I'm</u> scared.

1. *She is* happy.
2. *He is* angry.
3. *They are* bored.
4. *You are* hungry.
5. *I am* nervous.
6. *He is* serious.
7. *You are* sad.
8. *They are* thirsty.

Extra Practice

Ask six people what scares them. Write the answers, using contractions.

Example: He's scared of girls.   I'm scared of mice.

Unit 6

Introduction

1. The seven continents are North America, South America, Africa, Europe, Asia, Australia, and Antarctica. What two continents is Guatemala between?
2. Name two countries that border on Guatemala.
3. What is an ancient civilization?

Story

"The Maya in Guatemala" tells of an ancient civilization.

The Maya in Guatemala

In the country of Guatemala, there are many signs of the Mayan civilization. The Mayan culture began in 1000 B.C. Today there are two million Mayan Indians. There are still many people using the Mayan customs.

There are also many ruins from the Mayan days. There are the ruins in the city of Tikal. There are also large Mayan sites in the Peten region. There is the site Yaxja, there is the site of Ixcun, and there are many others. These places show the wonderful work of the Maya people.

There is also a book by the ancient Maya. It tells of Mayan traditions.

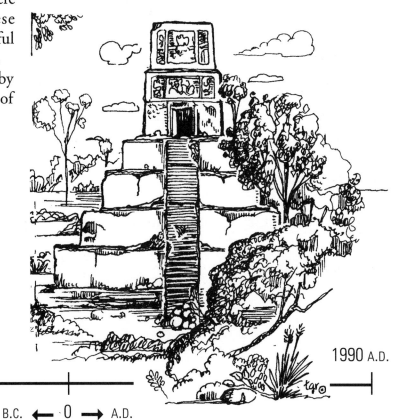

1000 B.C.

1990 A.D.

B.C. ← 0 → A.D.

Questions

1. When did the Mayan culture begin?
2. What city has Mayan ruins?
3. Would you like to visit the Mayan ruins?

Grammar Exercise

Study the grammar explanation. Then follow the directions.

There is/there are

• Use **there is** before singular nouns.
 	
• Use **there are** before plural nouns.
 	
                                        Singular (one)
    There   **is**   a book.
 	
                                          Plural (two or more)
    There   **are**   many ruins.

Directions: Copy each sentence. Replace the missing words with **There is** or **There are**. Mark the sentence as true or false, according to the story.

Example:	_____ signs of the Maya in Guatemala. **True** **False**
	There are signs of the Maya in Guatemala. True

1. _____ 20 million Maya Indians today.   **True**   **False**

2. _____ no one using the Mayan customs today.   **True**   **False**

3. _____ many ruins from the Mayan days.   **True**   **False**

4. _____ ruins in the city of Tikal.   **True**   **False**

5. _____ sites in the region of Peter Piper.   **True**   **False**

6. _____ the site of Yaxja.   **True**   **False**

7. _____ the site of Ixcun.   **True**   **False**

8. _____ a book by the ancient Maya.   **True**   **False**

Language Exercise

Read the information about numbers. Then follow the directions.

Cardinal Numbers					
1	one	20	twenty	1,000	one thousand
2	two	21	twenty-one	2,000	two thousand
3	three	22	twenty-two	↓	
4	four	↓		10,000	ten thousand
5	five	30	thirty	100,000	one hundred thousand
6	six	40	forty	1,000,000	one million
7	seven	50	fifty		
8	eight	60	sixty		
9	nine	70	seventy		
10	ten	80	eighty		
11	eleven	90	ninety		
12	twelve	100	one hundred		
13	thirteen	200	two hundred		
14	fourteen				
15	fifteen				
16	sixteen				
17	seventeen		1,848 = one thousand eight hundred forty-eight		
18	eighteen				
19	nineteen				

Directions: Copy the sentences. Replace each number with the words for the number.

> Example: The Mayan culture began in 1000 B.C.
> The Mayan culture began in one thousand B.C.

1. This culture was more than 3,000 years ago.
2. The Mayan civilization lasted for about 2,000 years.
3. The city of Tikal at one time had over 600,000 people.
4. The tallest temple in Tikal is 212 feet high.
5. Tikal was abandoned before 900 A.D.
6. The Mayan downfall was in 1542.

Extra Practice

Write the words for ten numbers in your life. For example, write the words for your address, your phone number, or your classroom number.

Unit 7

Introduction

1. The seven continents are North America, South America, Africa, Europe, Asia, Australia, and Antarctica. On which continent is South Korea?
2. Name two countries that border on South Korea.
3. What do you do on New Year's Day?

Story

"New Year's Day in South Korea" tells of a holiday in South Korea.

New Year's Day in South Korea

Carol: What is your favorite holiday in Korea?

Soonja: It is Sul Nal, or New Year's Day. But it is not on January 1. Sul Nal is on the first day of the first moon.

Carol: Are you busy that day?

Soonja: Yes, I'm very busy. We are awake early in the morning. The clothes of the children are bright in color. The boys and girls play games and fly kites. They're not bored for one moment. The men, women and children visit family and friends. They eat well. Most people give rice cakes and fruits to the spirits.

Carol: Are you tired at the end of the day?

Soonja: Yes, I'm tired, but happy.

Questions

1. When is New Year's Day in Korea?
2. What do people give to the spirits?
3. Do you play games on New Year's Day? Explain.

Grammar Exercise

Study the grammar explanation. Then follow the directions.

Negative: to be		
This is the form of the **present tense** of the verb *to be:*		

I	am not	
we you they	are not	happy
he she it	is not	

Examples: We *are not* happy. It *is not* on January 1.

Directions: Change each sentence to the negative form. Mark each new sentence as true or false, according to the story.

Example: New Year's Day is on January 1 in Korea.   True   False
New Year's Day <u>is not</u> on January 1 in Korea.   True

1. It is on the first day of the first moon.   **True   False**
2. "I am very busy during *Sul Nal,*" said Soonja.   **True   False**
3. "We are awake early in the morning," said Soonja.   **True   False**
4. The clothes of the children are bright in color.   **True   False**
5. The children are bored on this day.   **True   False**
6. The men, women, and children are hungry.   **True   False**
7. "I'm tired at the end of the day," said Soonja.   **True   False**
8. Soonja is happy on New Year's Day.   **True   False**

Language Exercise

Read the information about the spelling of plural nouns. Then follow the directions.

Spelling: Special Forms of Plural Nouns

Most nouns add *s* to make the plural. But some nouns have special plural forms.

SINGULAR	PLURAL	SINGULAR	PLURAL
child →	children	foot →	feet
man →	men	tooth →	teeth
woman →	women	mouse →	mice

Example: The *men, women,* and *children* visit family and friends.

Directions: Form the plurals of the following nouns:

1. tooth
2. man
3. child
4. mouse
5. foot
6. woman

Directions: Form the singular form of the following nouns:

1. men
2. women
3. feet
4. mice
5. children
6. teeth

Extra Practice

Answer the following questions using complete sentences.

1. How many teeth do you have?
2. How many children are in your family?
3. How many feet do you have?
4. How many men are in a dozen?

Unit 8

Introduction

1. The seven continents are North America, South America, Africa, Europe, Asia, Australia, and Antarctica. On which continent is Mexico?
2. Name two countries that border on Mexico.
3. Name a famous artist.

Story

"Frida Kahlo" is a biography of a famous artist from Mexico.

Frida Kahlo

Ann: I'm going to play a game with you. You guess the famous person.
Don: Okay. Is the person alive?
Ann: No, the person is not alive.
Don: Is the person a woman?
Ann: Yes, she is.
Don: Is she from North America?
Ann: Yes, she is.
Don: Is she from the United States?
Ann: No, she is not.
Don: Is she from Mexico?
Ann: Yes, she is.
Don: Is she an athlete or politician?
Ann: No, she is not an athlete or politician.
Don: Is she an author or an artist?
Ann: Yes, she's an artist.
Don: Is she a classical or modern artist?
Ann: She's a modern artist.
Don: Are her paintings in museums?
Ann: Yes, they are.
Don: Is her husband also a famous artist?
Ann: Yes, he is.
Don: I know! Is the person Frida Kahlo?
Ann: Yes, you're right!

Questions

1. Where is the artist from?
2. Where are her paintings now?
3. Do you like art?

Grammar Exercise

Study the grammar explanation. Then follow the directions.

Questions and Short Answers: to be						
Questions			Short Answers			
Am	I		Yes,	I	am.	
Is	she he it	famous?		he she it	is.	
Are	we you they			we you they	are.	
			No,	I	am not.	
				he she it	is not.	
Example: Is she famous? Yes, she is.				we you they	are not.	

Directions: Rewrite each sentence as a question. Then answer the question according to the story.

> Example: She is famous
>   Is she famous? Yes, she is.

1. She is North American.

2. She is Canadian.

3. She is alive.

4. She is an athlete.

5. She is an artist.

6. Her paintings are in museums.

7. Her paintings are classical.

8. Her husband is famous, too.

9. The woman is Frida Kahlo.

Language Exercise

Read the information about cursive writing. Then follow the directions.

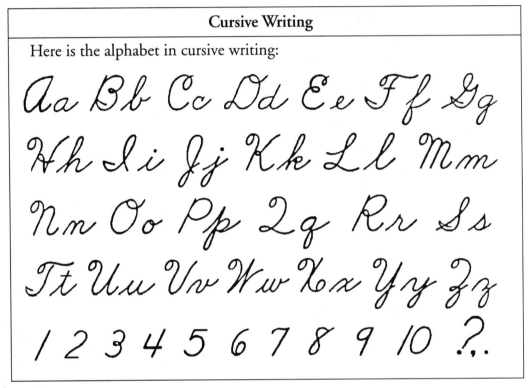

Cursive Writing

Here is the alphabet in cursive writing:

Directions: Copy the paragraph below in cursive writing.

Frida Kahlo is a Mexican artist. Her paintings are famous. Many of her works are self-portraits. Her art is surrealistic and romantic. She was married to Diego Rivera. Rivera is a famous mural painter. Kahlo died in 1954 at the age of 47.

Extra Practice

In cursive writing, describe a famous artist.

Unit 9

Introduction

1. On which continent is China?
2. Name two countries that border on China.
3. Tell about a famous place you know. Why is it famous?

Story

"The Great Wall of China" tells of a famous place in China.

The Great Wall of China

The Great Wall is in China. It is 1,500 miles long. It is the longest wall in the world. The wall begins near the Yellow Sea. It ends in the west in Gansu. The Great Wall was made more than 2,000 years ago.

The Great Wall is made of dirt, stone, and brick. It is 15 to 30 feet high. It is also very wide. Many people visit the Great Wall.

One visitor from the United States is James Williams. Every year Dr. Williams visits China. He studies medicine in Beijing. Dr. Williams always visits the Great Wall. He likes to walk on the wall. He takes pictures of the wall, too.

Questions

1. How long is the Great Wall?
2. When was the Great Wall made?
3. Do you want to visit the Great Wall? Why or why not?

Grammar Exercise

Study the grammar rules. Then follow the directions.

Verbs: Third Person Singular
Forming the third person singular tense: • Use the third person singular with singular nouns and the pronouns **he**, **she**, and **it**. • Add *s* to the verb to form the third person singular.

Third Person Singular		
The wall	begins	near the Yellow Sea.
It	ends	in Gansu.
He	walks	on the Great Wall.

Directions: Choose the verb that completes the sentence correctly. The correct sentences are also true sentences from the story.

> **Example:**   The wall (begin) (begins) near the Yellow Sea.
> The wall _begins_ near the Yellow Sea.

1. Dr. Williams (lives) (visits) in the United States.

2. The wall (end) (ends) in the west in Gansu.

3. James Williams (lives) (visits) China.

4. Dr. Williams (studies) (teaches) medicine in China.

5. The doctor always (visit) (visits) the 1,500-mile wall.

6. Dr. Williams (lives) (walks) on the Great Wall.

7. The doctor (take) (takes) pictures of the wall, too.

Language Exercise

Read the information about capitalization. Then follow the directions.

Capitalization: Names of Places

Capitalize the names of places, such as the names of cities, countries, continents, rivers, seas, and oceans.
 	
Examples:
 	
    Beijing   Yellow Sea   Gansu
 	
    Asia   China   Japan
 	
    Great Wall   India   Pacific Ocean
 	
    Ganges River North Korea   South Korea

Directions: Copy these sentences. Capitalize the names of places. See the example and look at the map for help.

> **Example:**   The country of china is in asia.
> The country of China is in Asia.

1. The great wall is not in japan.

2. The great wall begins near the yellow sea.

3. The great wall ends in gansu.

4. The city of beijing is in china.

5. The country of china is north of the country of india.

6. The pacific ocean is east of china.

7. The atlantic ocean is not near the country of japan.

8. There is a north korea and a south korea.

9. The ganges river is in the country of india.

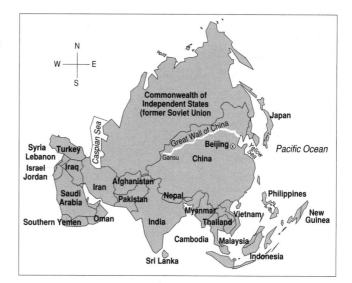

Extra Practice

Look at the map. Write sentences about the places on the map.

Unit 10

Introduction

1. The seven continents are North America, South America, Africa, Europe, Asia, Australia, and Antarctica. On which continent is Lithuania?
2. Name two countries that border on Lithuania.
3. What is a ghost?

Story

"A Ghost at the Door" is a story from Lithuania.

A Ghost at the Door

One night, a man and his wife were asleep. Suddenly, there was a knock at their door. "Let me in! Let me in!" said a voice.

"Who is it?" asked the wife. No one answered. The man and his wife were afraid. They did not open the door.

The next morning, the house was a mess. "What happened to our house! Look at my clothes!" said the wife.

"Look at my papers!" said the man.

That night, the knock came again.

"Who are you? What is your problem?" asked the man.

"Why do you have my shoes? Now I want two pairs of shoes!" said the voice.

"It's your uncle!" cried the woman. "Remember, we have his shoes!"

The man and woman found two pairs of shoes. They put the shoes on the uncle's grave.

At last the ghost has its shoes.

Questions

1. Who is the ghost?
2. What do the man and woman have?
3. Do you believe in ghosts?

Grammar Exercise

Study the grammar explanation. Then follow the directions.

Possessive Adjectives
Here are the personal pronouns and their corresponding possessive adjectives:

I	→	my	You have **my** shoes.
he	→	his	The man and **his** wife were asleep.
she	→	her	**Her** house was a mess.
it	→	its	The ghost wanted **its** shoes.
we	→	our	What happened to **our** house?
you	→	your	What is **your** problem?
they	→	their	They did not open **their** door.

Directions: Copy each sentence. Replace the missing word with the corresponding possessive adjective. Mark the sentence as yes (in the story) or no (not in the story).

Example: (he) A man and _____ wife were asleep.   **Yes**   **No**
A man and _his_ wife were asleep.   Yes

1. (they) There was a knock at _____ door.   **Yes**   **No**

2. (she) The woman opened _____ door.   **Yes**   **No**

3. (we) "What happened to _____ house?" asked the woman.   **Yes**   **No**

4. (I) "Look at _____ clothes!" said the ghost.   **Yes**   **No**

5. (I) "Look at _____ papers!" said the uncle.   **Yes**   **No**

6. (you) "What is _____ problem?" asked the man.   **Yes**   **No**

7. (you) "It's _____ aunt!" said the woman.   **Yes**   **No**

8. (it) At last the ghost has _____ shoes.   **Yes**   **No**

Language Exercise

Read the information about end marks. Then follow the directions.

Punctuation: End Marks

• **Period** (.) Use a period at the end of a sentence.
 	
    Example: The ghost is happy.
 	
• **Question mark** (?) Use a question mark at the end of a question.
 	
    Example: Who is it?
 	
• **Exclamation point** (!) Use an exclamation point to add emphasis or to show emotion.
 	
    Example: Let me in!

Directions: Copy the sentences. Use the correct end mark.

> Example: Who is it__
>   Who is it?

1. Let me in__

2. They were afraid__

3. What happened to our house__

4. Look at my clothes__

5. Who are you__

6. What is your problem__

7. It's your uncle__

8. We have his shoes__

9. They put the shoes on his grave__

10. At last the ghost has its shoes__

Unit 11

Introduction

1. What continent is the United Kingdom near?
2. Name the four divisions of the United Kingdom.
3. What is a chimpanzee?

Story

"Jane Goodall" is a biography of a famous scientist from England in the United Kingdom.

Jane Goodall

Jane Goodall is one of Africa's most outstanding scientists. For many years she has studied chimpanzees. Jane's books give information about these animals. Goodall also works to protect the lives of chimpanzees.

Jane Goodall was born in London, England. Her dream was to go to Africa. She became a secretary for a scientist in Kenya. The scientist's name was Louis Leakey. Leakey's guidance was important to Jane. With Leakey's help, Jane began to work with chimpanzees. Jane studied chimpanzees in Tanganyika for many years. Goodall is the winner of many awards. Jane's prizes include the Golden Medal of Conservation and the Order of the Golden Ark.

Questions

1. What animal does Jane Goodall study?
2. Who helped Jane?
3. Do you like chimpanzees? Why or why not?

Grammar Exercise

Study the grammar explanation. Then follow the directions.

Possessive Form of Nouns
With singular nouns, use an apostrophe + **s** to show possession.
the book of Jane   =   Jane's book
the help of Leakey   =   Leakey's help
Example: Jane**'s** books are about chimpanzees.

Directions: Copy each sentence. Replace the underlined words with the possessive form. Mark the sentence as true or false, according to the story.

> Example: Jane Goodall is one of <u>Africa scientists.</u>   **True**   **False**
>   Jane Goodall is one of <u>Africa's scientists.</u>   True

1. <u>Jane books</u> give information on gorillas.   **True**   **False**
2. <u>Ms. Goodall work</u> is to protect the lives of chimpanzees.   **True**   **False**
3. The <u>woman home</u> is Antarctica.   **True**   **False**
4. <u>Jane dream</u> was to go to Africa.   **True**   **False**
5. Jane became a <u>scientist secretary.</u>   **True**   **False**
6. The <u>scientist name</u> was Louis Leakey.   **True**   **False**
7. <u>Leakey guidance</u> was no help to Jane.   **True**   **False**
8. Jane <u>Goodall prizes</u> include the Nobel Peace Prize.   **True**   **False**

Language Exercise

Read the information about *this, that, these,* and *those.* Then follow the directions.

This, That, These, and Those

- Use the demonstrative adjectives **this**, **that**, **these**, and **those** to emphasize a noun.

- Use **this** and **these** with things that are near.

  (**this**—singular nouns; **these**—plural nouns)

- Use **that** and **these** with things that are far.

  (**that**—singular nouns; **those**—plural nouns)

	NEAR	FAR
Singular	this	that
Plural	these	those

Examples: I want **this** book and **these** tapes right here.

I want **that** chair and **those** desks over there.

Directions: Use **this** or **these**.

1. _____ scientist
2. _____ chimpanzees
3. _____ lives
4. _____ dream

5. _____ secretary
6. _____ names
7. _____ year
8. _____ divisions

Directions: Use **that** or **those**.

1. _____ continent
2. _____ books
3. _____ winner
4. _____ awards

5. _____ animals
6. _____ medal
7. _____ prizes
8. _____ information

Extra Practice

Describe ten objects in your room or classroom using **this**, **these**, **that**, **those**.

Examples: this book, that pencil, these pennies, those papers

Unit 12

Introduction

1. On which continent is Germany?
2. Name two countries that border on Germany.
3. What is a fortress?

Story

"The Stahleck Fortress" is about a famous place in Germany.

The Stahleck Fortress

The Rhine is an important river in Germany. It is also the longest river in Western Europe. Many boats travel on the Rhine. Tourists enjoy visiting the Rhine.

One interesting place on the Rhine is the Stahleck fortress. The building is very old. It was built in 1253. The Stahleck fortress is between two towns. The town of Oberwesel is above Stahleck on the map. The town of Bacharach is below the Stahleck fortress. The town of Bacharach is from the 1300s. Today the Stahleck fortress is a youth hostel. A youth hostel is a hotel for young people. Travelers can stay in the hostel overnight.

The Stahleck Fortress

Questions

1. When was the Stahleck fortress built?
2. What is the fortress today?
3. Would you like to travel in Europe and stay in youth hostels? Explain.

Grammar Exercise

Study the grammar explanation. Then follow the directions.

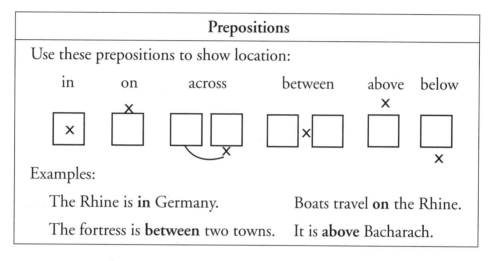

Examples:

The Rhine is **in** Germany.   Boats travel **on** the Rhine.

The fortress is **between** two towns.   It is **above** Bacharach.

Directions: Copy each sentence. Use the preposition in the picture. Mark the sentence as true or false, according to the story.

Example: Boats travel ⎡×⎤ the Rhine.   **True   False**
                   Boats travel <u>in</u> the Rhine.   False

1. The Rhine is an important river ☐ Germany.   **True   False**

2. The Stahleck fortress is ☐×☐ the Rhine.   **True   False**

3. The Stahleck fortress is ☐ two towns.   **True   False**

4. The town of Oberwesel is ☐×☐ Stahleck.   **True   False**

5. The Stahleck fortress is ☐×☐ two towns.   **True   False**

6. The town of Bacharach is ☐ the Stahleck fortress.   **True   False**

7. Young people can stay ☐×☐ the fortress.   **True   False**

8. The hostel ☐☐ the fortress.   **True   False**

Language Exercise

Read the information about directions. Then complete the exercise.

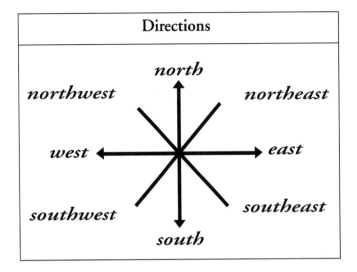

Directions

Directions: Look at the map of the Rhine River in Germany. Answer the questions.

1. What city is in the northeast corner of the map?

2. What city is in the northwest corner of the map?

3. Find Wiesbaden in the southeast corner. What city is north of Wiesbaden?

4. In the east, find the city of Wirges. What city is northeast of Wirges?

5. Burg Stahleck, or the Stahleck Fortress, is on the Rhine River in the southwest. What city is north of Burg Stahleck?

6. What direction does the Rhine (Rheim) River run: north to south or east to west?

Extra Practice

Draw a map of your home and neighborhood. Describe the area.

Examples: North of my house is Wilson Street. Southwest of my house is a drugstore.

The Rhine

Unit 13

Introduction

1. On which continent is Canada?
2. Name one country that borders on Canada.
3. Describe Eskimos, another name for Inuit.

Story

"The Inuit of Canada" is about the native people of Canada.

The Inuit of Canada

The Inuit are natives of Canada. (Many people use the name "Eskimos" for the Inuit.) The Inuit live near the Arctic Circle. There are 20,000 Inuit in Canada.

A long time ago, the Inuit lived by hunting animals. They always traveled on dogsleds. They usually lived in igloos of snow during the winter. Families came together to make small communities. Then in the summer, they usually lived in tents. They always dressed in furs of animals.

Today, the Inuit rarely travel by dogsleds. They have snowmobiles now. Also, the people live in regular houses. The students usually leave their communities to go to high school.

The Inuit are famous for their artwork. They carve figures of people and animals. The Inuit sometimes sell their art.

Questions

1. Describe the Inuit a long time ago.
2. Describe the Inuit today.
3. Would you like to live near the Arctic Circle? Explain.

Grammar Exercise

Study the grammar explanation. Then follow the directions.

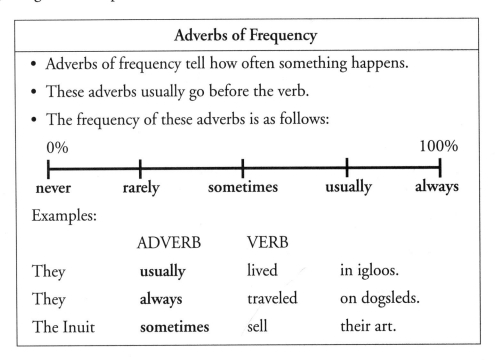

Directions: Write these sentences. Include the adverbs in parentheses ( ). Mark the sentence as true or false, according to the story.

Example: (never) People use the name Eskimos for the Inuit.   **True   False**
           People _never_ use the name Eskimos for the Inuit.   False

1. (rarely) The Inuit live near the Arctic Circle.   **True   False**
2. (always) Years ago, the Inuit traveled on dogsleds.   **True   False**
3. (usually) Years ago, the Inuit lived in igloos of snow.   **True   False**
4. (sometimes) Years ago, the Inuit lived in tents in the summer.   **True   False**
5. (rarely) Years ago, the Inuit dressed in furs of animals.   **True   False**
6. (always) Today, the Inuit travel by dogsleds.   **True   False**
7. (usually) The students leave their communities to go to high school.   **True   False**
8. (never) The Inuit sell their art.   **True   False**

Language Exercise

Read the information about spelling. Then follow the directions.

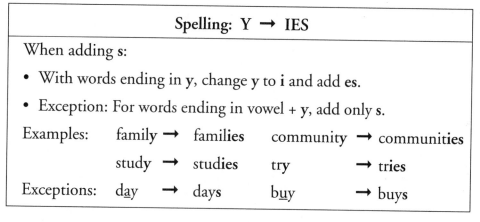

Spelling: Y → IES
When adding **s**:
• With words ending in **y**, change **y** to **i** and add **es**.
• Exception: For words ending in vowel + **y**, add only **s**.
Examples: family → families   community → communities
study → studies   try   → tries
Exceptions: d<u>a</u>y → days   b<u>uy</u>   → buys

Directions: Change the singular words to plural.

> Example: party____
>   part<u>ies</u>

1. family____
2. city____
3. study____
4. try____
5. baby____
6. story____
7. day____
8. community____
9. buy____

Extra Practice

Find eight more words that end in y. Change the words to plural form. (Use your dictionary or textbook to find words.)

Unit 14

Introduction

1. What continent is Sri Lanka near?
2. Name two countries that are near Sri Lanka.
3. What is a festival?

Story

"The Festival of Lights" is a Hindu holiday in Sri Lanka.

The Festival of Lights

Maria is visiting the home of Anya in Sri Lanka. She is asking Anya questions about the holiday. The family's religion is Hinduism. Everyone is preparing for the Hindu holiday called Diwali. The holiday is in autumn.

Maria: What holiday are you celebrating?

Anya: We're celebrating Diwali, the Festival of Lights.

Maria: What is your family doing?

Anya: We're cleaning the house. Lakshimi is going to visit us. Lakshimi is the goddess of good luck.

Maria: What is your father doing?

Anya: He's lighting our house. Then Lakshimi can find us. All the people are lighting their homes tonight.

Maria: What are you eating?

Anya: I'm eating a special candy. The candy is for this holiday. Do you want one?

Maria: Yes, thank you. It's delicious!

Questions:

1. What religion is Anya?
2. What is the family doing to prepare for the Festival of Lights?
3. What do you know about the Hindu religion?

Grammar Exercise

Study the grammar explanation. Then follow the directions.

Verbs: Present Continuous
• Use the **present continuous tense** to describe an action that is happening *now*.
• The **present continuous** is the verb **to be + present participle** (verb + ing).

Examples:	TO BE	VERB + ING	
I	'm	eating.	
We	're	cleaning	the house.
He	is	lighting	the home.
They	are	preparing	for the day.

Directions: Copy each sentence. Change the verb in parentheses ( ) to **present continuous tense**. Mark the sentence as true or false, according to the story.

Example: Maria _____ (visit) a home in Puerto Rico.   True   False
Maria _is visiting_ a home in Puerto Rico.   False

1. Maria _____ (ask) Anya questions about the holiday.   True   False
2. Everyone _____ (prepare) for the holiday called Epiphany.   True   False
3. Anya: We _____ (celebrate) Diwali.   True   False
4. Anya: We _____ (clean) the streets.   True   False
5. Anya: Lakshimi _____ (go) to visit us.   True   False
6. Anya: My father _____ (light) the church.   True   False
7. Anya: All the people _____ (light) their homes tonight.   True   False
8. Anya: I _____ (eat) a special candy.   True   False

Language Exercise

Read the information about spelling. Then follow the directions.

Spelling: Dropping e before -ing
• Before adding **-ing** to words that end in **-e**, drop the **e**. Examples: make ➡ making   prepare ➡ preparing   like ➡ liking   hope ➡ hoping

Directions: Copy the story about the Festival of Lights. Add **-ing** to the verbs in parentheses ( ). Remember to drop the **e** with words ending in **-e**.

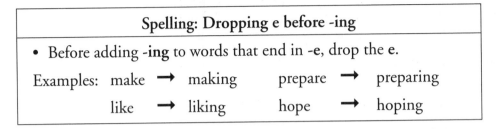

Example: The people who are (live) in Sri Lanka are happy today.
                The people who are <u>living</u> in Sri Lanka are happy today.

(1) The people who are (live) in Sri Lanka are happy today. (2) Everyone is (prepare) for the Festival of Lights. (3) They are (clean) their homes. (4) Lakshimi is (come) to the town. (5) The lights in the houses will be (guide) Lakshimi's way. (6) People are (hope) for good luck. (7) The families are (make) special candy. (8) They are (shape) the candy into animals and flowers. (9) The children are (wait) for the candy.

Extra Practice

Finish these sentences the way you want:

I am making _____. She is coming _____. They are hoping for _____. We are living _____. They are preparing for _____.

Unit 15

Introduction

1. On which continent is India?
2. Name two countries that border on India.
3. What does "good sense" mean?

Story

"The Lion Makers" is a story from India.

The Lion Makers

In a certain town there were four friends. Three of the friends had many years of schooling. Bharata had only good sense. "Let's travel. We can make money," said the first friend.

"Great. Let's go today," said the second friend.

"Go home, Bharata. We need smart men for this trip," said the third friend.

"No, don't go, Bharata. You're our friend," said the first friend.

The four friends went on their trip. In a forest, they found the bones of a lion. "Let's use our education," said the second friend. "Let's bring the lion to life."

"All right. I can fix the bones," said the third friend.

"I can fix the blood and skin," said the first friend.

"Don't bring the lion to life," said Bharata. "It is a lion. It will kill us."

"Don't listen to the fool. He knows nothing," said the third friend.

"Then wait a moment. I want to climb this tree," said Bharata. The three friends fixed the lion. The lion came to life. Then it killed all three men. The lion went away. Bharata climbed down the tree and went home.

School is important. But it is also important to have good sense.

Questions

1. Describe the four friends.
2. Bharata said, "Don't bring the lion to life." Why?
3. Do you have only education, only sense, or education and sense?

Grammar Exercise

Study the grammar explanation. Then follow the directions.

Verbs: Imperative
• The imperative is the base form of the verb.
• The imperative is used for commands and requests.
• "You" is not said. It is understood.
• Contractions: **let's** = let us; **don't** = do not

	AFFIRMATIVE (+)	NEGATIVE (-)
You	**Go** home.	**Don't go** home.
	Listen to him.	**Don't listen** to him.
We	**Let's go** home.	**Let's not** go home.
	Let's listen.	**Let's not listen.**

Directions: Change these **imperative** sentences to **negative** form. Mark the sentence as yes (in the story) or no (not in the story).

Example: *"Let's travel."*   **Yes**   **No**
              <u>"Let's not</u> travel."   No

1. *"Let's make* money."   **Yes**   **No**
2. *"Let's go* today."   **Yes**   **No**
3. *"Go,* Bharata. You're our friend," said the first friend.   **Yes**   **No**
4. *"Let's use* our education."   **Yes**   **No**
5. *"Let's bring* the lion to life," said the second friend.   **Yes**   **No**
6. *"Bring* the lion to life," said Bharata.   **Yes**   **No**
7. *"Listen* to the fool," said the third friend.   **Yes**   **No**
8. *"Wait* a moment," said Bharata.   **Yes**   **No**

Language Exercise

Read the information about education. Then follow the directions.

Vocabulary: Education
These are the names for the grades in school:

<u>Elementary School</u>   <u>High School</u>
Kindergarten   Grade 9 = freshman
Grades 1–6   Grade 10 = sophomore
                                                      Grade 11 = junior
                                                      Grade 12 = senior

<u>Middle School/Junior High School</u>   <u>College</u>
Grades 7–8

Directions: Match the school with the grade. Write the school and name for the high school grades.

Examples: grade 1 = _____   grade 9 = _____, _____
                  elementary school   high school, freshman

1. grade 6 = _____

2. grade 8 = _____

3. grade 10 = _____, _____

4. kindergarten = _____

5. grade 4 = _____

6. grade 12 = _____, _____

7. grade 7 = _____

8. grade 11 = _____

9. grade 5 = _____

10. after grade 12 = _____

Extra Practice

Write the name of the schools you or an adult attended.

Example: Ft. Lowell Elementary School; Townsend Junior High School;
                 Palo Verde High School; Southwestern College

Unit 16

Introduction

1. On which continent is Israel?
2. Name two countries that border on Israel.
3. Tell what you know about the Christian, Jewish, and Muslim religions. (These religions are called Christianity, Judaism, and Islam.)

Story

"The City of Jerusalem" tells about the capital of Israel.

The City of Jerusalem

Jerusalem is the capital of Israel. It is a holy city for three religions. These are the religions of Christianity, Judaism, and Islam.

In about 1000 B.C., King David made Jerusalem his capital. So he brought the Jewish religion to the city. From 37 B.C., the area was under Roman rule. During this rule, Jesus Christ (Christian leader) went to Jerusalem. He was killed there. Christianity later became the religion of the area. Then in 614 A.D., Jerusalem came under Muslim rule. Mohammed is the Muslim religious leader. Muslims say that Mohammed visited Jerusalem in the 600s.

Today, Judaism is the main religion in Jerusalem. But there are also Muslims and Christians living in the area. All religions have freedom of worship. All people can now visit their holy city of Jerusalem.

A Muslim mosque in Old Jerusalem

Questions

1. What three religions call Jerusalem their holy city?
2. What religious people live in Jerusalem today?
3. What is another religion in the world?

Grammar Exercise

Study the grammar explanation. Then follow the directions.

Conjunctions: and, but, or, because, so
• **Conjunctions** join words and parts of sentences together. Examples: Jews **and** Muslims live in Jerusalem. Christians live in Jerusalem, **but** more Jews live there. Are there more Christians **or** Muslims in Jerusalem? Jerusalem is important to Christians **because** of Jesus. Jerusalem is open, **so** all people can visit.

Directions: Join the two sentences together with the **conjunction** in parentheses ( ). Mark the sentence as true or false, according to the story.

Example: Jerusalem is the capital of Israel. (and) It is a holy city.   True   False
Jerusalem is the capital of Israel _and_ it is a holy city.   True

1. King David made Jerusalem his capital. (so) He brought the Muslim religion to the city.   **True   False**

2. Christians remember Jerusalem. (because) Jesus was killed there.   **True   False**

3. For awhile Christianity was the religion of the area. (but) It came under Muslim rule in 614 A.D.   **True   False**

4. Muslims feel Jerusalem is important. (because) Mohammed visited there.
True   False

5. Today, Judaism is the main religion in Jerusalem. (but) No other religious groups live there.   **True   False**

6. All religions have freedom of worship. (so) All people can visit Jerusalem.
True   False

Directions: Join the two questions together with the conjunction **or**. Then answer the questions.

Example:	Were Christians in Jerusalem first? (or) Were Jews in Jerusalem first?
	Were Christians in Jerusalem first or were Jews in Jerusalem first? Answer: Jews were in Jerusalem first.

1. Are there more Jews in Jerusalem? (or) Are there more Muslims in Jerusalem?

2. Were Jews in Jerusalem first? (or) Were Muslims in Jerusalem first?

Language Exercise

Read the information about **there** and **their**. Then follow the directions.

Confusing Words: Their/There
Their and **there** are pronounced the same, but they have different meanings and spellings.
• Use **their** for possession (belonging to *them*).
• **There** is an adverb.
Examples: Jerusalem is **their** city.   **There** is the city. Judaism is **their** religion.   Many people live **there**.

Directions: Write the sentences. Choose the correct word: **their** or **there**.

Example:	(Their) (There) is a holy city in Israel.
	<u>There</u> is a holy city in Israel.

1. In Israel, Judaism is (their) (there) religion.

2. King David made his capital (their) (there).

3. When Romans lived in Jerusalem, the city was under (their) (there) rule.

4. Jesus Christ was killed (their) (there).

5. For Muslims, Mohammed is (their) (there) religious leader.

6. Muslims say that Mohammed visited (their) (there).

Extra Practice

Use **there** in five sentences. Use **their** in five more sentences.

Unit 17

Introduction

1. On which continent is Russia?
2. Name two countries that border on Russia.
3. What is a cosmonaut?

Story

"Valentina Tereshkova" is a biography of a cosmonaut from Russia.

Valentina Tereshkova

Here are some questions and answers about Valentina Tereshkova.

Q: Who is Valentina Tereshkova?

A: She is a cosmonaut.

Q: Where is she from?

A: She is from Russia.

Q: What is a cosmonaut?

A: It is the Russian word for astronaut.

Q: Why is Tereshkova famous?

A: She was the first woman in space.

Q: When was her flight?

A: Her flight began on June 16, 1963.

Q: When did she return to earth?

A: She returned three days later.

Q: Where did she go?

A: She orbited around the earth.

Q: What was the name of her flight?

A: Vostok 6.

Q: When was Valentina born?

A: In 1937.

Q: What was her job before she was a cosmonaut?

A: She was a textile worker.

Valentina Tereshkova today

Questions

1. Why is Valentina Tereshkova famous?
2. When did she travel in space?
3. Would you like to be an astronaut? Explain.

Grammar Exercise

Study the grammar explanation. Then follow the directions.

Wh– Questions
• These words are used in asking questions: **who**   **what**   **when**   **where**   **why** Examples: **Who** is Valentina Tereshkova? **What** did she do? **When** was her flight? **Where** did Valentina go? **Why** is she famous?

Directions: Write the answers to these **Wh–** questions. Find the answers in the story.

1. Who was the first woman in space?

2. What country is she from?

3. Where did she go in space?

4. When did she go on her flight?

5. When did she return?

6. What was the name of her flight?

7. Why is Valentina famous?

8. When was she born?

9. What is a cosmonaut?

Language Exercise

Read the information about ordinal numbers. Then follow the directions.

Vocabulary: Ordinal Numbers

- **Ordinal numbers** indicate position in a series.
- Use **ordinal numbers** to write the date in words.

1st	first	11th	eleventh
2nd	second	12th	twelfth
3rd	third	13th	thirteenth
4th	fourth	14th	fourteenth
5th	fifth	15th	fifteenth
6th	sixth	16th	sixteenth
7th	seventh	17th	seventeenth
8th	eighth	18th	eighteenth
9th	ninth	19th	nineteenth
10th	tenth	20th	twentieth

Examples: Valentina was the **first** woman in space.
She returned to earth on the **third** day.
Valentina went in space on June **sixteenth**.

Directions: Change the **ordinal numbers** into words.

Example: 2nd _____
             second

1. 15th _____
2. 8th _____
3. 4th _____
4. 10th _____
5. 12th _____

6. 3rd _____
7. 1st _____
8. 9th _____
9. 7th _____
10. 6th _____

Directions: Look at the chart below on travel in space. Then answer the questions that follow.

SOVIET UNION SPACE FLIGHTS

Cosmonaut	Date	Event
Y. Gagarin	4/12/61	First manned space flight.
V. Tereshkova	6/16/63	First woman in space.
A. Leonov	3/18/65	First space walker.
G. Beregovoy	10/26/68	Met with Soyuz 2.
V. Shatalov	1/14/69	First docking of manned spacecraft.
A. Nikolayev	6/2/70	New record for number of hours in space.

Questions

1. Who was the first man in space?

2. When was the first space flight?

3. Who is the fifth person listed?

4. What is the sixth date listed?

5. Why is Leonov listed?

6. What happened on 10/26/68?

Extra Practice

Make a list of ten foods you like. Write your choices in ordinal numbers.

> **Examples:** My *first* choice is ice cream
> My *second* choice is cookies.
> My *third* choice is pizza.

Unit 18

Introduction

1. On which continent is Lebanon?
2. Name two countries that border on Lebanon.
3. Who is Mohammed in the Muslim religion?

Story

"Maulid an-Nabi" tells of a Muslim holiday in Lebanon.

Maulid an-Nabi

Many of the people in Lebanon are Muslim. They celebrate *Maulid an-Nabi,* Mohammed's birthday. Mohammed was the founder of the Islam religion. At the end of the year, there are nine days of celebration. Sam is asking Jahad about this special holiday.

Sam: What can you do on this holiday?

Jahad: We can listen to stories about Mohammed. My grandfather can tell a wonderful story about Mohammed's birth.

Sam: Can you tell me one story?

Jahad: Yes, I can. Seven thousand angels brought a vessel of dew to Mohammed's mother. The mother bathed Mohammed in the dew.

Sam: What activities can you do?

Jahad: We can go to the fairs. Also, everyone can watch the parades.

Sam: Can adults drink alcohol?

Jahad: No, people can't drink alcohol. It's not permitted.

Sam: Can you eat what you want?

Jahad: Yes, we can eat wonderful food. We eat dishes such as lamb, tabboul, and baklava for dessert.

Sam: Can you cook this food?

Jahad: No, I can't cook. But my parents can.

Questions

1. What activities are there during *Maulid an-Nabi*?
2. What food do the people eat during *Maulid an-Nabi*?
3. What part do you prefer of the *Maulid an-Nabi* celebration?

Grammar Exercise

Study the grammar explanation. Then follow the directions.

<table>
<tr><td colspan="4" align="center">Verbs: Can/Can't</td></tr>
<tr><td colspan="4">• Can't = can not</td></tr>
<tr><td colspan="4">• A verb usually follows can/can't.</td></tr>
<tr><td>Examples:</td><td>CAN/CAN'T</td><td>VERB</td><td></td></tr>
<tr><td>We</td><td>can</td><td>go</td><td>to fairs.</td></tr>
<tr><td>You</td><td>can</td><td>tell</td><td>a story.</td></tr>
<tr><td>I</td><td>can't</td><td>cook.</td><td></td></tr>
<tr><td>People</td><td>can't</td><td>drink</td><td>alcohol.</td></tr>
</table>

Directions: Copy each sentence. Choose **can** or **can't** to make the sentence correct according to the story.

> **Example:**   Jahad (can) (can't) tell Sam about *Maulid an-Nabi*.
>   Jahad _can_ tell Sam about Maulid an-Nabi.

1. Jahad: We (can) (can't) listen to stories about Mohammed.
2. Jahad's grandfather (can) (can't) tell a story about Mohammed's birth.
3. Jahad (can) (can't) tell a story about Mohammed.
4. During the holiday, people (can) (can't) go to fairs.
5. Also, everyone (can) (can't) see the parades.
6. People (can) (can't) drink alcohol.
7. Jahad: We (can) (can't) eat wonderful food.
8. Jahad: I (can) (can't) cook.
9. Jahad's parents (can) (can't) cook.

Language Exercise

Read the information about spelling. Then follow the directions.

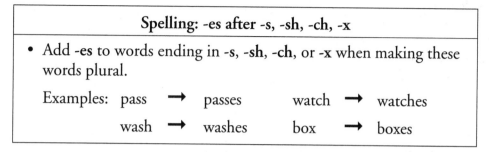

Spelling: -es after -s, -sh, -ch, -x
• Add **-es** to words ending in -s, -sh, -ch, or -x when making these words plural.
Examples: pass → passes   watch → watches
wash → washes   box → boxes

Directions: Copy the story about Mohammed's birth. Change the word in italics to its plural form.

> Example: When Mohammed is born, everyone *watch* the star over Mecca.
> When Mohammed is born, everyone <u>watches</u> the star over Mecca.

(1) When Mohammed is born, everyone *watch* the star over Mecca. (2) The King of the Seas *splash* the sea with its 7,000 tails. (3) A vessel *catch* dew. (4) The mother *get* the vessel from the 7,000 angels. (5) She *wash* the baby in the dew. (6) Everyone *march* many miles to visit Mohammed. (7) Everyone *shut* their eyes because of the child's bright face.

(8) Time *pass*. (9) When Mohammed is older, he *teach* people about the religion of Islam.

Extra Practice

How many watches, dresses, brushes, glasses, boxes, and sack lunches are in your classroom?

Unit 19

Introduction

1. In which ocean is Hawaii?
2. Name two continents near Hawaii.
3. What is a volcano?

Story

"Hawaii" tells about Hawaii, a state in the United States.

Hawaii

Sandy is asking Lanea about life in Hawaii.

Sandy: Does all of your family live in Hawaii?

Lanea: Yes, we do. Only my sister doesn't live here.

Sandy: Do you have volcanoes on your island?

Lanea: Yes, of course we do. All the islands of Hawaii are the tops of great volcanoes. I live on the big island called Hawaii. We have the world's largest active volcano. It's named Mauna Loa.

Sandy: Do you worry about living so close to an active volcano?

Lanea: No, we don't worry. The lava doesn't come to the towns.

Sandy: Do you have a good climate in Hawaii?

Lanea: Yes, we're famous for our climate. We swim in the ocean all year long. Also, the crops grow all year around. The two biggest crops are sugar and pineapples. I love the fresh fruits here.

Sandy: What fruits do you like best?

Lanea: I like pineapples and mangoes.

Sandy: What do you do for fun in Hawaii?

Lanea: Many people like to surf in the ocean. Sometimes we have parties. We cook outdoors and have a luau. Some girls can dance the hula.

Lumahai Beach, Kauai

Questions

1. What are the islands of Hawaii made of?
2. What do Hawaiians do for fun?
3. Would you like to visit Hawaii? Explain.

Grammar Exercise

Study the grammar explanation. Then follow the directions.

Negative: Simple Present

- **Do/does + not + base form** = negative of simple present
- Contractions: **doesn't** = does not; **don't** = do not

	DO/DOES + NOT	BASE	
I We You They	do not don't	live	in Hawaii.
He She It	does not doesn't	live	in Hawaii.

Examples: We **don't worry.**
            The lava **does not come** to the towns.

Directions: Change each verb in parentheses ( ) to the **negative simple present** form. Mark the sentence as true or false, according to the story.

Example: Lanea: We (live) in Hawaii.   **True**   **False**
               Lanea: We _don't live_ in Hawaii.   False

1. Lanea's sister (live) in Hawaii.   **True**   **False**
2. The Hawaiian Islands (have) volcanoes.   **True**   **False**
3. Lanea: I (live) on the big island called Hawaii.   **True**   **False**
4. The island of Hawaii (have) the world's largest active volcano.   **True**   **False**
5. The lava (come) to the towns in Hawaii.   **True**   **False**
6. Lanea: We (swim) in the ocean all year long.   **True**   **False**
7. Crops (grow) all year around.   **True**   **False**
8. Lanea: I (like) pineapples and mangoes.   **True**   **False**

Language Exercise

Read the information about spelling. Then follow the directions.

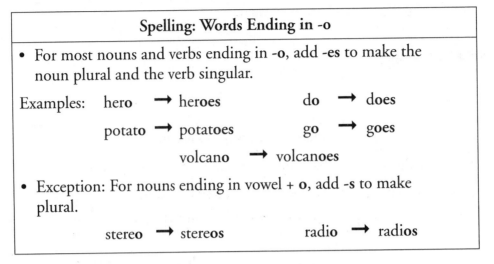

Spelling: Words Ending in -o

- For most nouns and verbs ending in -o, add -es to make the noun plural and the verb singular.

Examples: hero → heroes   do → does

potato → potatoes   go → goes

volcano → volcanoes

- Exception: For nouns ending in vowel + o, add -s to make plural.

stereo → stereos   radio → radios

Directions: Add -s or -es to the words below. Follow the rules on words ending in -o.

Example: zero
zeroes

1. do _____
2. volcano _____
3. radio _____
4. tomato _____
5. mango _____

6. stereo _____
7. go _____
8. studio _____
9. hero _____
10. rodeo _____

Extra Practice

Tell how many of these objects you have: radio, tomato, mango, potato, stereo, hero, studio.

Example: I have two radios, three tomatoes, zero studios.

Unit 20

Introduction

1. On which continent is Greece?
2. Name two countries that border on Greece.
3. What is a temple?

Story

"The Parthenon" tells about a famous temple in Greece.

The Parthenon

The Parthenon was made almost 2,500 years ago. This temple is in the city of Athens in Greece. The Parthenon is one of the most beautiful works of art from the ancient world. The builders used white marble to build the temple. The temple was for the goddess Athena.

Builders started the Parthenon in 447 B.C. The artist Phidias directed the work. Phidias made many works of art for the temple. His statue of Athena was very lovely. The statue was made of ivory and gold. In the 400s A.D., the Byzantines carried the statue to Constantinople. Then the statue disappeared forever.

For a thousand years, the Byzantines used the Parthenon as a Christian church. In the 1400s, the Turks used the temple as a mosque. In 1687, the Parthenon was mostly destroyed in an explosion.

In 1829, the Turks left Greece. Then the Greeks partly restored the Parthenon. Today the Parthenon is a favorite spot for tourists.

Questions:

1. For whom was the temple of the Parthenon built?
2. What mostly destroyed the temple?
3. Would you like to visit the Parthenon? Explain.

Grammar Exercise

Study the grammar explanation. Then follow the directions.

Verbs: Simple Past

• Use the **simple past** for actions in the past.
 	
• Add **-ed** to regular verbs.
 	
• If the verb ends in **-e**, add only **-d**.
 	
 VERB + **-ed**
Examples: The builders   start**ed**   the Parthenon.
 	
               Turks   used   the temple as a mosque.
 	
               The Greeks   restor**ed**   the temple.

Directions: Correctly complete the paragraphs on the Parthenon. Use the **past tense verbs** below.

Example: Builders <u>started</u> the Parthenon in 447 B.C.

used	protected	started	carried
restored	used	directed	disappeared
exploded			

(1) Builders _____ the Parthenon in 447 B.C. (2) The temple was for Athena because she _____ the Greeks. (3) Phidias _____ the work on the Parthenon. (4) Later, attackers _____ the statue of Athena to Constantinople. (5) The statue then _____ forever.

(6) For 1,000 years, the Byzantines _____ the Parthenon as a church. (7) Later the Turks _____ the temple as a mosque. (8) The building _____ in 1687. (9) After the Turks left, the Greeks _____ the Parthenon.

Language Exercise

Read the information about letter writing. Then follow the directions.

Letter Writing

Here is the form for a friendly letter:

Date

Dear _____,

xxxxxxxxxxxxxxxxxx
xxxxxxxxxxxxxxxxxxx
xxxxxxxxxxxxxxx.
      xxxxxxxxxxxxxxxxxx
xxxxxxxxxxxxx.

Yours truly,

Example:

8/27/93

Dear Diana,

I'm having a wonderful trip! I just visited Athens. My favorite part was the Parthenon. I really enjoyed the artwork.

Yours truly,

Directions: Write a friendly letter. Tell about a place you visited. Use the form below:

Date

Dear _____,

I'm having a wonderful vacation! I just visited _____. My favorite part was _____. I really enjoyed _____.

Yours truly,

Extra Practice

Write another letter to a friend. Write about what you are doing.

Unit 21

Introduction

1. On which continent is South Africa?
2. Name two countries that border on South Africa.
3. In the story "Unanana and the Elephant," there is a woman who risks death to save her children. Would you risk death to save your family? Explain.

Story

"Unanana and the Elephant" is a legend by the Zulus, a people from South Africa.

Unanana and the Elephant

Many years ago lived a woman named Unanana. She had two beautiful children with bright eyes.

One morning Unanana went into the bush to find wood. She left her two children with their cousin. Two hours later, the cousin saw a leopard. She and the children hid in the bush. "I can see you," said the leopard. "What lovely children!" The leopard walked away. He was not hungry.

At the end of the day, an elephant came by. The children and the cousin were afraid. "Oh, what beautiful children! I want them." The elephant ate the two children.

Soon Unanana came home. The cousin told her the terrible news. "Maybe the children are alive in the elephant's stomach," said Unanana. "I must find that elephant!"

Unanana took the wood, a pot, and a large knife with her. The leopard helped her find the elephant.

Unanana saw the elephant. "You took my children!" she said. "Where are they?" The elephant said nothing. He ate Unanana. Inside the elephant's stomach, Unanana saw many people, dogs, cows, and her two children.

Unanana made a fire. "Oh, I don't feel good!" said the elephant. Then he died. Quickly, Unanana cut a door in the elephant's stomach. Out walked the men, women, dogs, cows, and children. Unanana and her children were happy again.

Questions

1. What bad thing happened to the two children?
2. What did the mother do?
3. Is this story real? Explain.

Grammar Exercise

Study the grammar explanation. Then follow the directions.

Verbs: Irregular Past Tense			
• Many common verbs have special **past tense** forms.			

Examples:

PRESENT	PAST	PRESENT	PAST
come ➡	**came**	make ➡	**made**
cut ➡	**cut**	say ➡	**said**
eat ➡	**ate**	see ➡	**saw**
go ➡	**went**	take ➡	**took**
have ➡	**had**	hide ➡	**hid**
leave ➡	**left**		

Examples:

	PAST	
Unanana	**took**	the wood with her.
The cousin	**saw**	a leopard.

Directions: Change the verbs in parentheses ( ) to **past tense**. Mark the sentence as true or false, according to the story.

Example: Unanana (have) five beautiful children.   **True   False**
Unanana _had_ five beautiful children.   False

1. One morning Unanana (go) to find wood.   **True   False**
2. She (leave) her children with their uncle.   **True   False**
3. The cousin (see) a monkey.   **True   False**
4. The cousin and the children (hide) in a bush.   **True   False**
5. The elephant (eat) the two children.   **True   False**
6. Unanana (come) home in three days.   **True   False**
7. The cousin (tell) Unanana the terrible news.   **True   False**
8. Unanana (take) the wood, a pot, and a knife with her.   **True   False**

Language Exercise

Read the information about subjects and predicates. Then follow the directions.

Subject and Predicate
• Sentences consist of two parts: **Subject** 　– Subjects are the persons or things the sentence is about. 　– Subjects are nouns and pronouns. **Predicate** 　– Predicates tell something about the subject. 　– Predicates have verbs. Examples:　　SUBJECT　　　　　　PREDICATE 　　　　　　Unanana　　　　　　had two children. 　　　　　　She and the children　hid in the bush. 　　　　　　Slowly it　　　　　　walked away.

Directions: Copy each sentence. Underline the subject once and the predicate twice.

Example:　I can see the children.
　　　　　I can see the children.

1. The leopard walked away.
2. He was not hungry.
3. The children and the cousin were afraid.
4. I want them.
5. Maybe the children are alive in the elephant's stomach.
6. The leopard helped Unanana.
7. The elephant ate Unanana.
8. The children were happy to see their mother.
9. Everyone walked out of the elephant's stomach.

Extra Practice

Write ten sentences. Trade papers with a partner. Mark the subjects and predicates.

Unit 22

Introduction

1. On which continent is the Czech Republic?
2. Name two countries that border on the Czech Republic.
3. Havel fought against Communism. What is Communism?

Story

"Vaclav Havel" is a biography of a famous leader from the Czech Republic.

Vaclav Havel

Vaclav Havel is a famous leader from the Czech Republic. He became president of the country in 1989.

When Havel was young, Communists controlled Czechoslovakia. Russians took control of Czechoslovakia after World War II. Havel wanted to attend the university. He didn't go, though. The Communist government didn't permit him to go. Havel became a playwright. He wrote many famous plays. His plays attacked the government. In 1968, many Czechoslovakians wanted a different government. Communist armies came into Czechoslovakia. Havel and others were silenced. In 1977, 700 Czechoslovakian leaders signed a human rights paper. Havel was one of the leaders of this paper. The government didn't like the idea. Havel was jailed three times for his ideas.

Again in 1989, Czechoslovakian people protested the government. This time, the Communist government left. Havel became president. Czechoslovakia had their first free election in more than 40 years.

The Slovaks decided they wanted their own country. Havel didn't want the Slovaks to leave. But in 1993, there was a peaceful division. Czechoslovakia divided into the Czech Republic and the Slovak Republic. Havel became the Czech president.

Vaclav Havel

Questions

1. Who controlled Czechoslovakia after World War II?
2. Why is Havel famous?
3. Would you want to be president of your country? Explain.

Grammar Exercise

Study the grammar explanation. Then answer the questions.

Verbs: Negative Past Tense		
• Use **did not** + **base** form of verb to form negative past tense.		
• Did not = **didn't** (contraction)		

	DID NOT	BASE
I She He It We You They	did not didn't	go.

Examples:	DID NOT	BASE
He	did not	go.
The government	didn't like	the idea.
They	didn't want	to be one country.

Directions: Change the base verb in parentheses ( ) to the **negative past tense**. Mark the sentence as true or false, according to the story.

> Example: Communists (control) Czechoslovakia after World War II.
> Communists <u>didn't control</u> Czechoslovakia after World War II.
> False

1. Havel (go) to the university.   **True   False**

2. The Communist government (permit) Havel to go to the university.   **True   False**

3. Havel (write) many famous plays.   **True   False**

4. In 1968, Communist armies (come) into Czechoslovakia.   **True   False**

5. In 1977, 700 Czechoslovakian leaders (sign) a human rights paper.   **True   False**

6. The Communist government (like) the human rights paper.   **True   False**

7. Havel (go) to jail three times for his ideas.   **True   False**

8. In 1989, Czechoslovakians (protest) the government.   **True   False**

9. Havel (become) president of Czechoslovakia in 1989.   **True   False**

10. Havel (want) the Slovaks to leave the country.   **True   False**

Language Exercise

Read the information about antonyms. Then follow the directions.

Vocabulary: Antonyms
• Antonyms = opposite in meaning.
• An antonym is opposite in meaning to another word.

Examples of antonym pairs:

young	→	old
leader	→	follower
right	→	wrong

Directions: Choose the correct antonym for each word. Choose from the list below. (The antonyms are from the story "Vaclav Havel.")

Example: support _____
             protest

leader	free	different	attack	go	right
silence	like	protest	divide	peace	

1. same _____

2. defend _____

3. follower _____

4. war _____

5. noise _____

6. unite _____

7. come _____

8. controlled _____

9. dislike _____

10. wrong _____

Extra Practice

Write ten pairs of antonyms.

Examples: hot — cold

          sad — happy

Unit 23

Introduction

1. On which continent is Sweden?
2. Name two countries that are near Sweden.
3. In this story, the old king is afraid of claws. What are claws?

Story

"Linda-Gold and the Old King" is a story from Sweden.

Linda-Gold and the Old King

Long ago there was an old king. He was a little crazy. His family was killed by someone with claws. So he believed all people had claws. No one could touch the king. In all other ways, he was a good king. His people were sad because there weren't princes or princesses to follow the king.

One day the king was walking slowly through the forest. He saw a girl running from a wolf. The old king quickly killed the wolf.

"Oh, thank you! Please walk home with me. I'm afraid of more wolves." The little girl was pretty with golden hair.

The king walked home with the girl. "May I hold your hand?" asked Linda-Gold.

"No," said the king. "You have claws on your hands."

Linda-Gold was sad. "May I visit you tomorrow?"

The king said yes. The next day, Linda-Gold came to the castle. She smiled happily to see the king. The king liked Linda-Gold. The girl was sweet and kind. "Look, I cut my fingernails!" said Linda-Gold. "I don't have claws now. May I hold your hand?"

The king looked carefully. He didn't see any claws.

"All right, then," said the king. He held the girl's hand. He felt loved again.

The king told all the people, "Linda-Gold is our new princess!" The people were joyful.

Questions

1. Why couldn't people touch the king?
2. Why did the king feel loved again?
3. Would you like to be a prince or a princess? Explain.

Grammar Exercise

Study the grammar explanation. Then follow the directions.

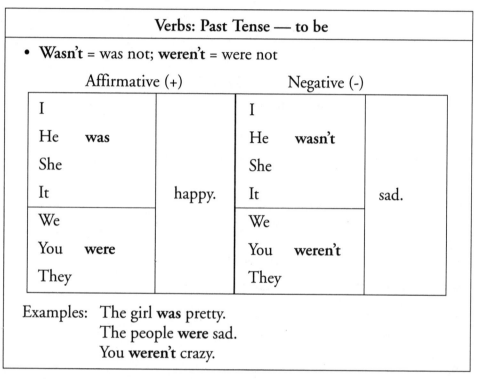

Verbs: Past Tense — to be			
• **Wasn't** = was not; **weren't** = were not			
Affirmative (+)		Negative (-)	
I He **was** She It	happy.	I He **wasn't** She It	sad.
We You **were** They		We You **weren't** They	
Examples: The girl **was** pretty. The people **were** sad. You **weren't** crazy.			

Directions: Choose **was, were, wasn't,** or **weren't** to complete the sentences correctly according to the story.

> **Example:**   Long ago there _____ an old king.
> Long ago there _was_ an old king.

1. The king's family _____ alive.
2. The king _____ right in the head.
3. In all other ways, he _____ a good king.
4. His people _____ happy.
5. There _____ princes and princesses to follow the king.
6. There _____ a wolf running after Linda-Gold.
7. The girl _____ big.

Language Exercise

Read the information about adjectives and adverbs. Then follow the directions.

Adjectives and Adverbs

• An **adjective** is a word that describes a noun.
 	
Examples: The girl was **pretty**.
                   The **small** girl ran.
                   The king was **crazy**.
 	
• An **adverb** is a word that generally describes a verb.
 	
• Many **adverbs** are formed by adding **-ly** to an adjective.
 	
Examples: The king walked **slowly**.
                   She smiled **happily**.
                   The king looked **carefully**.

Directions: Complete the sentences with the correct **adjective** or **adverb**.

> **Example:**   The king walked (slow) (slowly).
> The king walked <u>slowly.</u>

1. The king (quick) (quickly) killed the wolf.
2. The girl was (nervous) (nervously) about the wolves.
3. Linda-Gold was (sad) (sadly).
4. She smiled (happy) (happily) to see the king.
5. The girl was (sweet) (sweetly).
6. The king looked (careful) (carefully) at Linda-Gold.
7. Linda-Gold is the (new) (newly) princess.
8. The people were (joyful) (joyfully).

Extra Practice

Describe different events that you do *quickly, slowly, nervously, sadly, happily, carefully,* and *joyfully.*

> **Examples:** I walk quickly.   I do my homework slowly.
>   I nervously take tests.

Unit 24

Introduction

1. On which continent is Ghana?
2. Name two countries that border on Ghana.
3. What is a deer hunt?

Story

"Offering of the Deer" tells about a special festival in Ghana.

Offering of the Deer

In Ghana, there is a special festival held in April or May. It is called *Aboakyer.* This day is for hunting deer. The Effutu people of Ghana celebrate this day. They will make a deer offering to the god Panche Otu. They want the god to give them good luck all year.

Two groups will try to catch deer. In the groups are all ages. There will be young boys, men, and grandfathers. The men and boys will wear the bright colors of their group.

At sunrise, the drums will call to the groups. Then bells will ring and the village people will do a dance. The two groups go to hunt. They won't return until they find a deer. The men and boys will take the first deer back to the chief. The deer is still alive. Then the drums will beat louder and the dancers will dance faster.

This day is important for all the people. Everyone helps to make *Aboakyer* a lucky day.

Questions

1. Why do the Effutus make a deer offering to the god?
2. Who are in the two groups?
3. Which would you prefer to be: a drummer, a dancer, or a hunter? Explain.

Grammar Exercise

Study the grammar explanation. Then follow the directions.

Verbs: Future Tense
• **Will + base** form = **future tense.**
• Tomorrow, next week, next year, this Tuesday = time expressions that indicate future.
• Contractions: **I'll** = I will; **he'll** = he will; **she'll** = she will; **it'll** = it will; **we'll** = we will; **you'll** = you will; **they'll** = they will.
• Contraction: **won't** = will not.

	WILL/WILL NOT	BASE
I he she it we you they	will ('ll) will not (won't)	dance. be happy. ring the bells. return.

Examples:　**He'll** be happy.
　　　　　　They **won't** return tomorrow.
　　　　　　This day **will** be lucky.

Directions: Complete the sentences correctly with the future tense. Use the base words below:

take　　ring　　hunt　　try　　be　　give　　wear　　dance　　celebrate

> **Example:**　The Effutu people of Ghana _____ *Aboakyer.*
> The Effutu people of Ghana _will celebrate_ Aboakyer.

1. The Effutu _____ deer on this day.
2. The people hope the god _____ them good luck.
3. Two groups _____ to catch deer.

4. There _____ young boys, men, and grandfathers.

5. Everyone _____ the bright colors of their group.

6. The bells _____ after the drums call.

7. The village people _____ at sunrise.

8. The group _____ the first deer back to the chief.

Language Exercise

Read the information about contractions. Then follow the directions.

Vocabulary: Make/Do
• **Make** = build or create; usually, **make** = action with your hands.
• Use **make** with food, art, clothes, objects made by hand, a bed.
Examples: She **makes** dinner.
They will **make** an offering.
• **Do** = perform or finish
• Use **do** with a job, work, a show, a dance, homework.
Examples: They will **do** a dance.
She **does** her homework.

Directions: Choose the correct response from the following verbs: **make, makes, do, does**.

> **Example:**   They will _____ an offering to the god.
> They will *make an offering to the god.*

1. The women _____ the clothes for the men and boys.

2. The village people _____ a dance.

3. The boy _____ a picture of the deer.

4. The women will _____ the food for everyone.

5. Everyone _____ a good job.

6. We _____ our homework.

7. Roberto _____ things from wood.

8. She _____ her bed every day.

Extra Practice

Write five things you **make** and five things you **do**.

> **Examples:**   *I make my bed.   I make pictures.   I do my homework.*

Unit 25

Introduction

1. On which continent is Bolivia?
2. Name two countries that border on Bolivia.
3. In Bolivia, Ekeko is the god of prosperity. What does "prosperity" mean?

Story

"Alacitas" is a festival in Bolivia.

Alacitas

Lee is asking questions about Alacitas. This is a festival in Bolivia. It is celebrated by the Aymara Indians. Indians from all over Bolivia go to the city of La Paz for Alacitas.

Lee: What is the reason for the Alacitas festival?

Jose: The festival is for the god Ekeko. He is the god of prosperity. He brings us many good things.

Lee: When is the festival going to be?

Jose: The festival is going to be in January for three days.

Lee: What are the people going to do for the festival?

Jose: They are going to make figures of the god Ekeko. He is a little man with a big belly, an open mouth and open arms. He has a pack on his back.

Lee: What happens with the figures?

Jose: These figures of Ekeko guard the doors of homes. The people make miniature items of clothing, food, pots, and pans. They fill Ekeko's pack with these items and money. Then the people will have prosperity all year.

Lee: I know there is a big fair, too. What are people going to sell at the fair?

Jose: They are going to sell the figures and miniature items. People also sell beautiful wood carvings, rugs, and clothing of wool.

Questions

1. What is the reason for the Alacitas festival?
2. What happens at the fair?
3. What do you buy at fairs in your area?

Grammar Exercise

Study the grammar explanation. Then follow the directions.

Verbs: Future Using "Going to"			

- Another way to show the **future** is to use **am/is/are + going to + base.**

	AM/IS/ARE	GOING TO	BASE
I	am (not)		be.
He She It	is (not)	going to	do. sell.
We You They	are (not)		go.

Examples: I **am not going to go** to the fair.

She's **going to sell** the figures.

They **are going to make** miniature items.

Directions: Complete the sentences correctly with the **future tense** using "**going to.**" Use **going to** + the base words below:

sell	be	make	go	bring
guard	fill	be	make	have

> **Example:**   There is _____ a festival in Bolivia called Alacitas.
> There is _going to be_ a festival in Bolivia called Alacitas.

1. The Indians are _____ to La Paz to celebrate.

2. The god Ekeko is _____ many good things.

3. The festival is _____ in January.

4. The Indians are _____ figures of Ekeko.

5. The figures are _____ the doors of homes.

6. The people also are _____ miniature items.

7. The people are _____ Ekeko's pack with items and money.

8. Then the people are _____ prosperity all year.

9. The Indians are _____ wood carvings and rugs.

Language Exercise

Read the information about synonyms. Then follow the directions.

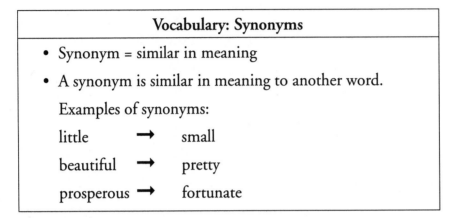

Vocabulary: Synonyms
• Synonym = similar in meaning
• A synonym is similar in meaning to another word.

Examples of synonyms:

little → small

beautiful → pretty

prosperous → fortunate

Directions: Choose the correct synonym for each word from the list below. (The synonyms are from the story "Alacitas.")

explanation	watch	town	large	bag
celebration	thing	little	stomach	pretty pots

Example: festival _____
celebration

1. city _____

2. miniature _____

3. reason _____

4. guard _____

5. belly _____

6. pack _____

7. beautiful _____

8. item _____

9. big _____

10. pans _____

Extra Practice

Write ten pairs of synonyms

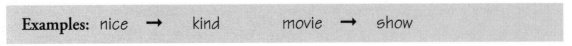

Examples: nice → kind   movie → show

Unit 26

Introduction

1. On which continent is Myanmar?
2. Name two countries that border on Myanmar.
3. What are a diplomat and a negotiator?

Story

"U Thant" is a biography of a famous diplomat from Myanmar (formerly Burma).

U Thant

Here are some questions and answers about the world famous diplomat from Burma. (Burma is now called Myanmar.)

Q: Are you familiar with U Thant?

A: Yes, I am. He was the Secretary-General of the United Nations from 1961 to 1971.

Q: Is he still alive?

A: No, he isn't. He was born in 1909 and died in 1974.

Q: Was he part of the Cuban missile crisis in 1962?

A: Yes, he was a negotiator during the crisis. He also was part of the peace negotiations in Indonesia (1962), the Congo (1963), Cyprus (1964), and the India-Pakistan war (1965).

Q: Was he in favor of nuclear arms?

A: No, he was against nuclear arms. He wanted the United States and the Soviet Union to stop nuclear arms.

Q: Was his first name "U"?

A: No, "U" is similar to "Mr." The name Thant means pure or clean. Many people from his country have only one name.

Questions

1. Why is U Thant famous?
2. What was his opinion on nuclear arms?
3. Would you like to be a diplomat? Explain.

Grammar Exercise

Study the grammar explanation. Then follow the directions.

Questions: Present and Past Tense "to Be"

- To form questions with *to be,* reverse the **subject** with the **verb.**

PRESENT			PAST		
Am	I			I	
Is	he / she / it	famous?	Was	he / she / it	famous?
Are	we / you / they		Were	we / you / they	

Examples: **Am I** from the United Nations?
Are they diplomats?
Were you from Myanmar?

Directions: Write these words in the correct order to form questions. Then answer the questions according to the story.

Example: familiar / you / are / with U Thant / ?
Are you familiar with U Thant? Yes, I am.

1. was / a famous diplomat / U Thant / ?
2. U Thant / was / of the United Nations / Secretary-General / ?
3. still alive / is / U Thant / ?
4. U Thant / was / of the / part / Cuban missile crisis?
5. was / a negotiator / U Thant / during the Cuban crisis / ?
6. part of the peace negotiations / was / U Thant / in Indonesia / ?
7. was / part of the 1978 crisis / U Thant / ?
8. in favor / was / he / of nuclear arms / ?

Language Exercise

Read the information about abbreviations. Then follow the directions.

Abbreviations
• Abbreviation = a short form of the word or phrase.

Here are some abbreviations and their meanings:

Mr.	= mister	Thurs.	= Thursday
Mrs.	= married woman	Fri.	= Friday
Ms.	= single/married woman	Sat.	= Saturday
Mon.	= Monday	Sun.	= Sunday
Tues.	= Tuesday	U.N.	= United Nations
Wed.	= Wednesday	U.S.	= United States

Directions: Write the **abbreviations** for the following words.

Example: Thursday _____
Thurs.

1. Friday _____
2. Saturday _____
3. Sunday _____
4. married woman _____

5. single/married woman
6. mister _____
7. United Nations _____
8. Monday _____

Directions: Write the words for the following **abbreviations**.

Example: Sun. _____
Sunday

1. Mon. _____
2. Tues. _____
3. Wed. _____
4. Thurs. _____

5. Fri. _____
6. Sat. _____
7. U.N. _____
8. Mr. _____

Extra Practice

Find six abbreviations in a newspaper or magazine. Write these abbreviations and their meanings.

Example: St. = street   N. = north

Unit 27

Introduction

1. On which continent is Brazil?
2. Name two countries that border on Brazil.
3. This story is about a turtle and a leopard. Tell the similarities and differences between a turtle and a leopard.

Story

"Jabuti and the Leopard" is a story from Brazil.

Jabuti and the Leopard

The Leopard always wanted to catch Jabuti. Jabuti, the turtle was slower than the leopard. But Jabuti was smarter than the Leopard. Many times Jabuti escaped death.

This time Jabuti was asleep. Leopard found him. "Now, I have you!" said the Leopard. "I'm going to kill you at last. But I am a fair animal. I'll let you decide the way."

"Share your ideas with me," said Jabuti. "Then I'll choose my death."

"I can drop you on a rock," said the Leopard.

"No," said Jabuti. "That's impossible. You can't hurt my tough shell."

"Then I'll put you in the ground," said the Leopard.

"That won't work," said Jabuti. "The rain will come. Then I can get out of the ground."

"Well," said the Leopard impatiently, "I'll throw you in the river."

"Oh, no!" cried Jabuti. The turtle looked very unhappy. "Not the river! I'll die!"

The Leopard threw the turtle in the river. Shortly, the turtle's head appeared.

"Ha, ha!" Jabuti laughed. "I'm an excellent swimmer. Did you know that?" The turtle swam far away from the Leopard.

Questions

1. Name the ways that the Leopard wanted to kill the turtle.
2. Why did Jabuti say he would die in the river?
3. Which do you think is the smartest of all the animals? Explain.

Grammar Exercise

Study the grammar explanation. Then follow the directions.

Direct Object
• A **direct object** takes the action of the verb.
• A **direct object** usually follows the verb.

Examples:

	VERB	DIRECT OBJECT	
The Leopard	found	**the turtle.**	
I'll	throw	**you**	in the river.
You	decide	**the way.**	

• These **object pronouns** are used as objects of verbs or prepositions:

me	us
you	them
him, her, it	

Directions: Write these sentences in the correct word order, according to the story. Underline the direct object.

> Example: Jabuti / the Leopard / wants to catch.
> The Leopard wants to catch Jabuti.

1. the turtle / many times / death / escaped.
2. going to kill / I'm / at last / you.
3. your ideas / share / with me.
4. I'll / my death / choose.
5. on a rock / you / I / can drop.
6. You / my tough shell / can't hurt.
7. in the ground / I / will put / you.
8. I / will throw / in the river / you.

Language Exercise

Read the information about prefixes. Then follow the directions.

Prefixes: Un-, Il-, Im-, In-
• The prefixes **un-**, **il-**, **im-**, and **in-** = not
• Unhappy = not happy; **illegal** = not legal

Examples

UN-	IL-	IM-	IN-
unable	illegal	impatient	inaccurate
unclear	illogical	imperfect	indirect
unequal		impossible	indecent
unhappy			
unlucky			

That's **impossible**," said Jabuti.

The turtle looked very **unhappy**.

Directions: Make the following words negative by adding the prefix **un-**, **il-**, **im-**, or **in-**.

Example: equal ——
             unequal

1. patient _____
2. happy _____
3. accurate _____
4. logical _____
5. decent _____

6. perfect _____
7. clear _____
8. direct _____
9. legal _____
10. lucky _____

Extra Practice

Choose five words beginning with the prefixes **un-**, **il-**, **im-**, or **in-**. Write a story using these words.

Unit 28

Introduction

1. On which continent is the United States?
2. Name two countries that border on the United States.
3. "Paul Bunyan" is a tall tale. What is a tall tale?

Story

"Paul Bunyan" is the hero of an American tall tale.

Paul Bunyan

Paul Bunyan was born in the state of Maine. When he was a baby, he picked up cows. At two years old, he was bigger than a house, smarter than five men, and stronger than a bull. His father was a logger. Mr. Bunyan cut down trees and sold them. Paul wanted to help his father. He went to his neighbor's yard. He found one of the better trees. Then he pulled the tree out. The neighbors didn't like Paul.

Paul's family decided to move to a quieter place. They went west to Michigan. Paul grew taller than the trees. As a young man, he ran faster than a deer. He also could fight harder than a bear. He had a good friend. His friend was Babe, a blue ox.

When Paul was older, he moved to Oregon. Babe went with him. Paul started a logging camp. He had armies of men to help him. The cooks made huge pancakes to give the men. Each pancake was bigger than a house.

Paul and Babe went up north to see Alaska. Maybe they are still there. People say you can hear Paul laughing in the mountains on a clear day.

Questions

1. Is "Paul Bunyan" a true story? Explain.
2. Name two unusual things about Paul Bunyan.
3. What is your favorite line from the story? Explain.

Grammar Exercise

Study the grammar explanation. Then follow the directions.

Comparison: Comparative Form of Adjectives
• To compare two things, use this form with short adjectives: **adjective + -er + than** • **Good** → better in the comparative form. • **Big** → bigger in the comparative form. Examples: Paul was **bigger than** a house. This is **quieter than** the other place. Paul was **taller than** the trees.

Directions: Write the **comparative form** of the adjective in parentheses ( ). Then mark the sentences about the story as true or false.

Example: (big) At two years old, Paul was _____ than a mountain. **True   False**
At two years old, Paul was <u>bigger</u> than a mountain.   False

1. (smart) At two years old, Paul was _____ than twenty men.   **True   False**

2. (strong) At two years old, Paul was _____ than an elephant.   **True   False**

3. (good) Paul found one of the _____ cows in his neighbor's yard.   **True   False**

4. (quiet) Paul's family wanted to move to a _____ place.   **True   False**

5. (tall) Paul grew _____ than the mountains.   **True   False**

6. (fast) He ran _____ than a deer.   **True   False**

7. (hard) He could fight _____ than a bear.   **True   False**

8. (old) When Paul was _____ he moved to Ohio.   **True   False**

9. (big) The pancakes were _____ than a house.   **True   False**

Language Exercise

Read the information about abbreviations. Then follow the directions.

State Abbreviations

- These are the **abbreviations** for the fifty states in the United States.
- Note that there is no period following the **abbreviations**.

Alabama	AL	Kansas	KS	Ohio	OH
Alaska	AK	Kentucky	KY	Oklahoma	OK
Arizona	AZ	Louisiana	LA	Oregon	OR
Arkansas	AR	Maine	ME	Pennsylvania	PA
American Samoa	AS	Maryland	MD	Puerto Rico	PR
California	CA	Massachusetts	MA	Rhode Island	RI
Canal Zone	CZ	Michigan	MI	South Carolina	SC
Colorado	CO	Minnesota	MN	South Dakota	SD
Connecticut	CT	Mississippi	MS	Tennessee	TN
Delaware	DE	Missouri	MO	Trust Territories	TT
District of Columbia	DC	Montana	MT	Texas	TX
Florida	FL	Nebraska	NE	Utah	UT
Georgia	GA	Nevada	NV	Vermont	VT
Guam	GU	New Hampshire	NH	Virginia	VA
Hawaii	HI	New Jersey	NJ	Virgin Islands	VI
Idaho	ID	New Mexico	NM	Washington	WA
Illinois	IL	New York	NY	West Virginia	WV
Indiana	IN	North Carolina	NC	Wisconsin	WI
Iowa	IA	North Dakota	ND	Wyoming	WY

Directions: Below is a map of Paul Bunyan's travels across the United States. List the states that Paul traveled through. (Use the complete names and the abbreviations.)

Example: Maine, ME

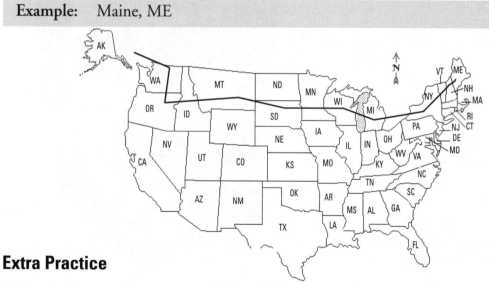

Extra Practice

Write the names of ten states and their abbreviations that you would like to visit.

Example: California, CA   New York, NY

Unit 29

Introduction

1. On which continent is Colombia?
2. Name two countries that border on Colombia.
3. What is the Nobel Prize for Literature?

Story

"Gabriel Garcia Marquez" is a biography of a famous writer from Colombia.

Gabriel Garcia Marquez

Here are questions and answers about Gabriel Garcia Marquez, the famous author from Colombia.

Q: Gabriel Garcia Marquez was born in Colombia in 1928. Did he stay there?

A: He stayed in Colombia for awhile. He attended the University of Bogota. Later he worked as a reporter for a Colombian newspaper.

Q: Why did he leave his country?

A: Garcia Marquez became a foreign correspondent in Rome, Paris, Barcelona, and New York. He has lived mostly in Mexico and Europe.

Q: What is his most famous book?

A: His most famous novel is <u>One Hundred Years of Solitude</u>. It was published in 1968. The novel has sold more than 10 million copies. It also is translated into thirty-two languages.

Q: When did Garcia Marquez receive the Nobel Prize for Literature?

A: He received the prize in 1982.

Q: Did he write other books?

A: Yes, he has written many popular novels and short stories.

Questions

1. Why is Garcia Marquez famous?
2. How popular is his novel <u>One Hundred Years of Solitude</u>?
3. Would you like to be an author? Explain.

Grammar Exercise

Study the grammar explanation. Then follow the directions.

Questions: Past Tense			
• To form past tense questions, use **did** + **subject** + **base** form of verb.			
• Question words such as **who, what, when, where, why, how,** and **how many** go before **did** in past tense questions.			
QUESTION WORDS	DID	SUBJECT	BASE
	Did	**they**	**stay** there?
Why	did	Gabriel	leave his country?
When	did	he	receive the Nobel Prize?

Directions: Write these words in the correct order to form questions. Then answer the questions according to the story.

Example: Garcia Marquez / did / stay / in Colombia?
Did Garcia Marquez stay in Colombia?   No, he didn't.

1. did / what university / Garcia Marquez / attend?

2. he / where / did / work first?

3. leave / his country / he / did / why?

4. he / work / where / did / in Europe?

5. live mostly / where / did / he?

6. in 1968 / what / he / write / did?

7. did / Garcia Marquez / how many copies / sell?

8. receive / did / what prize / he?

9. other books / he / did / write?

Language Exercise

Read the information about capitalization. Then follow the directions.

Capitalization: Titles
• Capitalize the first word and other important words in a title.
• Don't capitalize words in titles like **the**, **a**, **an**, **and**, **of**, **in**, **on**, **with**, **at**, **to**.
• Titles include names of books, stories, magazines, movies, and songs. Examples: One Hundred Years of Solitude   Romeo and Juliet

Directions: Copy these book titles by Gabriel Garcia Marquez. Capitalize as needed and underline the titles.

Example: one hundred years of solitude
                  One Hundred Years of Solitude

1. no one writes to the colonel and other stories
2. the autumn of the patriarch
3. innocent erendira and other stories
4. in evil hour
5. leaf storm and other stories
6. love in the time of cholera

Extra Practice

Write ten titles of your favorite books, magazines, movies, stories, and songs. Use correct capitalization.

Unit 30

Introduction

1. Which continent is Jamaica near?
2. Name two countries that are near Jamaica.
3. What is prejudice?

Story

"Little Kitten and Little Rat" is a story from Jamaica.

Little Kitten and Little Rat

Once upon a time Little Kitten and Little Rat were best friends. They loved to play together. First Little Kitten ran after Little Rat. Then Little Rat ran after Little Kitten. They laughed at their games. They also loved to explore the jungle. At the end of the day, they were very tired. They rested together on a spot of sand.

That evening, Mother Rat asked, "Did you have a good day? What were you doing?"

Little Rat answered, "I was playing with my friend Little Kitten."

"What! You were playing with a cat! Oh no, you must not do that. Cats like to eat rats! You have to play with other rats."

That same evening, Mother Cat asked, "Little Kitten, you are very tired. What were you doing today?"

"I was playing with my friend Little Rat," answered Little Kitten.

"I can't believe that! Kittens don't play with rats. Kittens like to eat rats," said Mother Cat.

The next day, Little Rat and Little Kitten went to their favorite place. They looked at each other. Then they talked about their mothers' advice.

"I think we shouldn't play. We can't be friends now," said Little Rat.

"I believe you are right. We have to play with our own kind," said Little Kitten.

"Good-by. We should never meet again." The two left, both very sad.

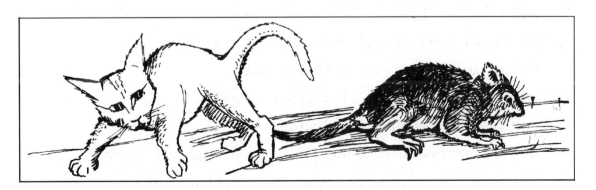

Questions

1. Why did the mothers tell Little Kitten and Little Rat not to play together?
2. This story tells about the way prejudice begins. Explain.
3. How can we solve the problem of prejudice?

Grammar Exercise

Study the grammar explanation. Then follow the directions.

Helping Verbs: Can, Should, Have to, Must

- A **main verb** expresses action or being.
- A **helping verb** helps complete the meaning of the main verb.
- Some common **helping verbs** include **can, should, have to, must.**

	HELPING VERB	MAIN VERB	
You	**must**	**do**	that.
I	**can't**	**believe**	it.
We	**shouldn't**	**play**	together.

Examples: We **have to** play with our own kind.
We **should** never meet again.

Directions: Copy each sentence. Complete the sentence with the correct helping verb according to the story.

> **Example:** Mother Rat said, "You (must) (must not) play with a cat."
> Mother Rat said, "You <u>must not</u> play with a cat."

1. Mother Rat said, "You (can't) (have to) play with other rats."
2. Mother Cat said, "I (can) (can't) believe that you played with a cat!"
3. "Kittens (must) (shouldn't) play with rats," said Mother Cat.
4. "Kittens (can) (can't) eat rats," said Mother Cat.
5. Little Rat said, "We (have to) (shouldn't) play together."
6. Little Rat said, "We (must) (can't) be friends now."
7. "We (have to) (shouldn't) play with our own kind," said Little Kitten.
8. "We (should) (shouldn't) see each other again," said Little Kitten.

Language Exercise

Read the information about clustering. Then follow the directions.

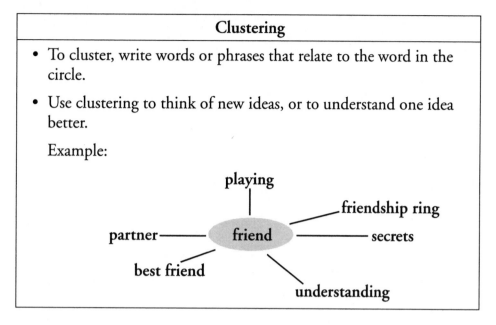

Directions: Make a cluster of the word "prejudice." Think of words that relate to "prejudice." You can use synonyms, people, actions, things, and so on.

Extra Practice

Make a cluster of the word "kitten." Then make a cluster of the word "rat." Compare your two clusters.

Grammar/Language Index

Unit	Grammar	Language
1	Verbs: simple present	Capitalization: first word in a sentence
2	Personal pronouns	Indentation
3	Nouns: singular and plural	Alphabetical order
4	Indefinite articles: a / an	Writing the date
5	Verb: to be	Contractions: to be
6	There is / there are	Vocabulary: cardinal numbers
7	Negative: to be	Spelling: irregular plural nouns
8	Questions and short answers: to be	Cursive writing
9	Verbs: third personal singular	Capitalization: names of places
10	Possessive adjectives	Punctuation: end marks
11	Nouns: possessive forms	Demonstrative adjectives: this / that / these / those
12	Prepositions	Vocabulary: directions on a map
13	Adverbs of frequency	Spelling: $y \rightarrow ies$
14	Verbs: present continuous	Dropping e before -ing
15	Verbs: imperative	Vocabulary: education
16	Conjunctions: and, but, or, because, so	Confusing words: their / there
17	Wh– questions	Vocabulary: ordinal numbers
18	Verbs: can / can't	Spelling: -es after -s, -sh, -ch, -x
19	Negative: simple present	Spelling: plural of words ending in -o
20	Verbs: simple past	Letter writing

Unit	Grammar	Language
21	Verbs: irregular past tense	Sentences: subject and predicate
22	Verbs: negative past tense	Vocabulary: antonyms
23	Verbs: past tense "to be"	Parts of speech: adjectives and adverbs
24	Verbs: future tense	Vocabulary: make / do
25	Verbs: future using "going to"	Vocabulary: synonyms
26	Questions: present and past tense "to be"	Abbreviations
27	Direct object	Prefixes: *un-, il-, im-, in-*
28	Comparison: comparative form of adjectives	Abbreviations of states in the U.S.
29	Questions: past tense	Capitalization: titles
30	Helping verbs: can, should, have to, must	Clustering